Feng Shui in 10 Simple Lessons

Feng Shui in 10 simple lessons

JANE BUTLER-BIGGS

AURUM PRESS

I dedicate this book to my children Alexei, Josef and Imogen
and to the generation to which they belong, who form the future for us all.

Published in Great Britain
2000 by Aurum Press Ltd
25 Bedford Avenue, London WC1B 3AT

A catalogue record for this book is available from the British Library.

ISBN 1 85410 695 3

This book was conceived, designed, and produced by

THE IVY PRESS LTD

The Old Candlemakers

West Street, Lewes

East Sussex BN7 2NZ

Creative Director: PETER BRIDGEWATER
Designers: PAUL ELMES, HELEN HARRIS
Editorial Director: SOPHIE COLLINS
Managing Editor: ANNE TOWNLEY
Project Editor: LORRAINE TURNER
Editor: ANNETTE DE SAULLES
Studio Photography: IAN PARSONS
Illustrations: KEVIN O'BRIEN, ANDREW KULMAN, JANE TATTERSFIELD
Three-Dimensional Images: CHRIS MANSBRIDGE
Picture Research: VANESSA FLETCHER

Reproduction and printing in China by
Hong Kong Graphic and Printing Ltd

This book is typeset in 10/14 Gill Sans Light

調節空間

contents

Introduction

I have written this book as a "Welcome back", or a chance to remember some of the things that we and our ancestors have always known, but that may have become a little obscured in the rush and alienation of current times.

As you read it, you should feel a sense of recognizing truths that some part of you always knew, a way of being that for some time has lain in neglect. People that I have taught over the years have often reported a sense of release and relief, of 'coming home' as once again the door is opened on a practice that they instinctively know can be an incredibly powerful tool to be used in every facet of their lives.

Feng Shui, as I have always practised it, is a way of empowering and supporting individuals in their daily experiences of life. It no longer needs to be a tool held in the hands of the all-knowing expert, a fixed set of rules to be carried out slavishly by passive and disempowered individuals who hardly dare to understand, much less question, the mystical utterances and awesome calculations of the grand masters. It can be a living and breathing practice, rooted in close observation and a heightened awareness of the presence and impact of the energy, or life force, in ourselves and the space around us.

To practise Feng Shui in such a way that an absolute distinction between good and bad directs our every action is to keep fear and separation as the motivating structures in our lives. The approach taught in this book is a reflection of my practice as a teacher and

ABOVE **Thoughtful positioning of ornaments, pictures and flowers can enhance the positive energy in your home.**

LEFT **Feng Shui can help you through all stages of moving home, from choosing where to live and planning the move, to arranging the decor and furnishings.**

序

consultant, working from a position of trust in the natural order of life, that allows growth and change in such a way that difficulty turns into challenge, challenge into opportunity and opportunity into pure delight.

Everyone has a part to play in this practice, each person bringing his or her own agenda and level of commitment at any one time, each person experiencing Feng Shui practice and the transformation it can bring.

By understanding the way the process works, and experiencing the changes each action creates, Feng Shui becomes a natural part of our daily experience. We can then work with energy in the same way that our ancestors worked, with the desire to understand more about the nature of energy so that we can move in an increasingly harmonious way with the natural order of things. The first people to practise Feng Shui understood that to be in tune was to be aligned with life so that clarity and the ability to change and act when necessary came naturally to each person as part of a harmonious whole.

By returning to a way of practice that acknowledges the power in experiencing life from moment to moment, we can allow the teaching of past practitioners and philosophers to support, rather than disempower, our current practice of Feng Shui and put us in a position to take it forward in a useful and constructive way.

This book was written in a spirit of trust, joy and enlightenment. These will be the gifts that anyone reading it will receive, that anyone practising Feng Shui in this way will enjoy.

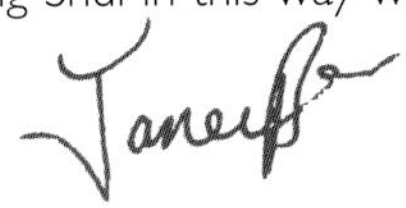

Janey

JANE BUTLER-BIGGS

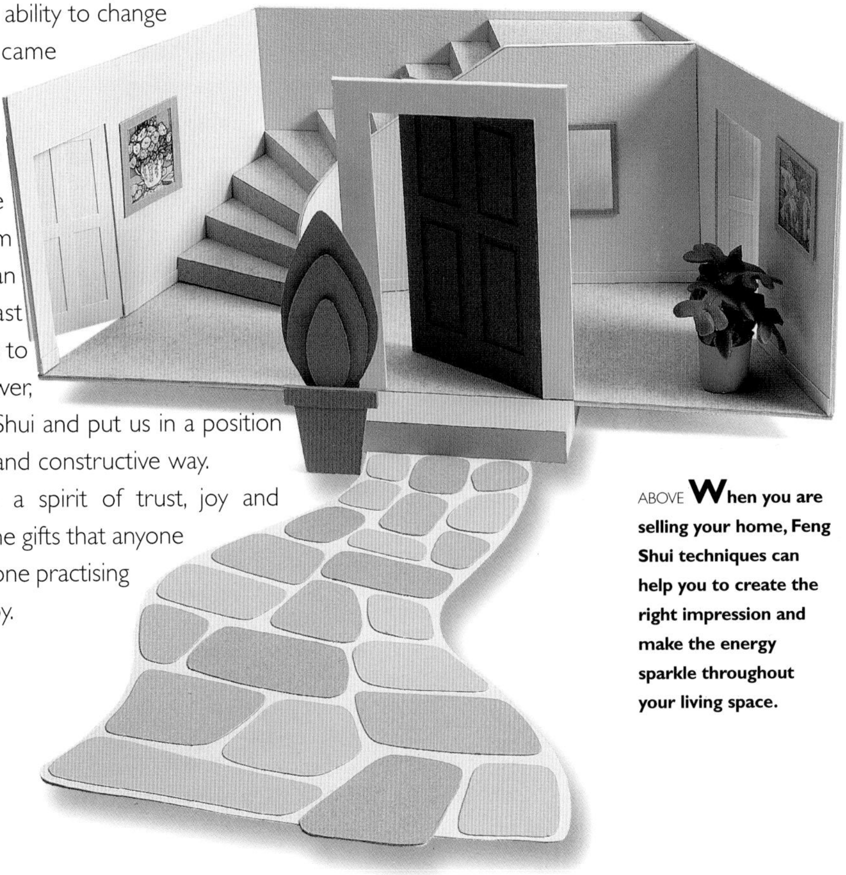

ABOVE **When you are selling your home, Feng Shui techniques can help you to create the right impression and make the energy sparkle throughout your living space.**

7

I

grasping the basics

The practice of Feng Shui can help us to improve our lives simply by increasing awareness of our surroundings and the energy we let into our bodies. Energy is present everywhere, from the atmosphere surrounding us to the food we eat. If we decide to live on a diet of doughnuts and soda, for example, it will affect our physical wellbeing. Likewise, if we accept second best in our choice of living arrangements, the atmosphere surrounding us will be second rate, and perhaps even detrimental to our physical and emotional health.

WHY YOU NEED FENG SHUI

Those of us who have taken time out to understand the energetics of food are already in a position to make certain choices. We know, for example, that it is better to cut the amount of saturated fat in our diet, and to increase our consumption of fresh fruit and vegetables. We know our diet makes a difference to our energy levels, health, performance at work and at home – in short, to our happiness levels and what we may read as our good luck. So it is important to become more aware of what we are taking into our system.

Now, try to extend this awareness of energy into your surroundings. What do you see, smell, hear and feel happening around you? Try to sense what kind of energy is surrounding you. For example, we all know that being in a place where we remember having an argument with a loved one reminds us of feeling bad, but what about less obvious connections – a long time spent in a cold room, say? Bad experiences, even seemingly trivial ones, will not help our emotional and physical wellbeing, so it is important both to be aware of them and, wherever possible, to take control of them.

LEFT **In a busy world, Feng Shui can help you to rearrange your environment in order to improve your lifestyle and increase your control over the events that occur in your life.**

BELOW **It is good Feng Shui practice to be aware of the energy we are taking into our bodies, including the energy we get from food. A balanced diet should include lots of fresh fruit and vegetables for optimum health.**

LEFT **S**plashes of red in the bathroom are stimulating and invigorating, and will help people to feel wide awake and energized before going to work.

TAKING RESPONSIBILITY

In order to improve our lives, we need to take responsibility for initiating change. If we decide that there is nothing much we can do to become happier, more successful, more content, then these things are unlikely to occur. We need to be able to see why things happen, and how events and our environment affect us.

TAKING CHARGE

We can start by looking at our environment for clues about what is going on in our lives and why. In order to do this, we need to examine why certain features have a particular effect on us. Instead of simply saying things like "I don't like red rooms", we should try to clarify our feelings further. For example, we could say "I don't like red rooms because I can't relax in them". Once we realize that red makes it harder for us to relax, we may begin to see the advantages of using red in a situation where we need more energy. For example, if you need to boost your confidence at work in order to impress a new boss, you could add a few touches of red to your bathroom, which will invigorate you before a day's work.

By learning to read your environment, you can begin to understand how it influences your life, and then you can decide whether or not you would like to make changes.

So Feng Shui can be applied every day. Very often it gives us the life-changing insight that allows things to fall into their rightful place.

ABOVE **C**utting down on 'fast foods' such as hamburgers and chips, and increasing our intake of home-cooked meals, will improve our health and enable us to spend more time enjoying meals with our loved ones.

BASIC FENG SHUI

Feng Shui involves increasing our awareness of our surroundings, taking more responsibility for improving our lives, knowing when to take action, and learning how to enjoy the best of things. Practising the art of Feng Shui is an ongoing process of learning to live with your space. This process is sometimes slow and sometimes fast but, like choosing what to wear, or who to see, it is an exciting and rewarding part of being alive.

WHO USES FENG SHUI?

BELOW **Feng Shui involves making decisions about our surroundings to get the best out of a situation, such as choosing a relaxing place like a park to have your lunch-break.**

To a greater or lesser degree, everybody already practises Feng Shui. For example, if you step onto a train and choose where to sit, or if you walk into your office and rearrange some files so that you can sit down more comfortably, you are negotiating your space. If you watch people getting onto a bus or a train, you will notice that most of the passengers will be actively choosing their seats and their positions in relation to each other.

ABOVE **C**hoosing which clothes to wear for particular situations is the kind of Feng Shui adjustment that most people practise unconsciously. Both colour and style have the ability to influence the wearer's mood.

MAKING ADJUSTMENTS

If you know exactly why you are making particular movements and are aware of their repercussions, then you are consciously practising Feng Shui. Here are some of the low-level adjustments we commonly make to our space:

■ "I want to sit alone so that I can work."

■ "I want to sit amongst people so that I have something to watch and listen to; I need some stimulation."

■ "I need more room on my desk so that I can think more clearly."

These are all low-level Feng Shui adjustments. Some people take it a step further:

■ "In a meeting, which chair should I pick to increase my power?"

■ "Where should I eat my lunch today, because I need to relax?"

Practising Feng Shui at this level is clearly appropriate for everybody every day – perhaps exams have been passed, or deals clinched, on the strength of choosing the right chair.

THE NEXT STEP

Once we appreciate the powerful connections between features of our living space and the impact they have on our lives, we can progress from the realms of low-level Feng Shui to level two, Keynote Feng Shui, where we ask ourselves questions such as:

"How can I rearrange my house so that more people come to see me, or so that I sleep better?"

"How can I set up my office so that I feel less tired?"

Keynote Feng Shui is using Feng Shui to set up a beneficial environment, which will change your life at a deeper level. Everyone can use Feng Shui successfully in this way.

Very soon you will get to the stage where as well as assessing your house to see how it impacts on your life, you will take much broader landscape features into account – perhaps you will look out of your window and wonder just why you are living so close to a big oak tree or looming tower block. At this point you will have arrived at level three.

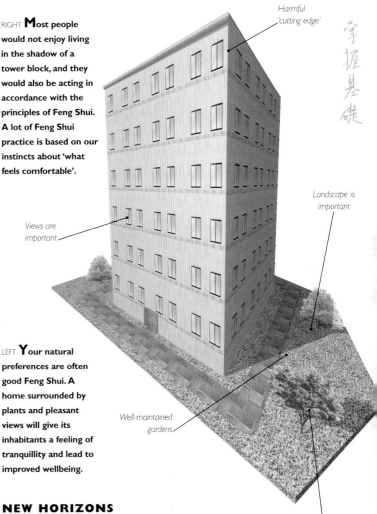

RIGHT **Most people would not enjoy living in the shadow of a tower block, and they would also be acting in accordance with the principles of Feng Shui. A lot of Feng Shui practice is based on our instincts about 'what feels comfortable'.**

Harmful 'cutting edge'

Landscape is important

Views are important

Healthy trees

Well-maintained gardens

LEFT **Your natural preferences are often good Feng Shui. A home surrounded by plants and pleasant views will give its inhabitants a feeling of tranquillity and lead to improved wellbeing.**

NEW HORIZONS

At level three, we can ask wider-ranging questions:

"Why am I in this space rather than any other?"

"How is this location affecting me and what would happen if I changed it – and how would I change it?"

Looking at your location will answer some of your broader questions about your life, and matching your location to your specific needs will open up completely new horizons.

Countless people have learnt how to do this and the fact that you have picked up this book and are reading it right now means that, should you wish to, you can do this too.

LEFT **Chi is an invisible force that is present everywhere. It moves more freely in wide, open spaces, which is why the clean air of the countryside often feels so invigorating.**

WHAT IS CHI?

The Chinese regard chi (pronounced 'chee') as the most important aspect of Feng Shui. Chi is an invisible energy that runs through all things. In order to live well, we need to encourage a healthy flow of this force around us, and prevent it from stagnating. How we arrange our homes and workplaces is therefore very important.

Find out about the state of the chi in your environment by asking yourself some simple questions. What do you see? What do you hear? What do you feel? What do you smell, and taste? Different spaces can actually create different tastes in your mouth. Make sure you are breathing freely and naturally. Aim to interact with the environment, but allow yourself to be open-minded and learn what the place has to tell you. Ask yourself: "What could I happily do here? Could I relax, celebrate, do a day's work, make love?" In other words, what sort of energy does this space have?

Energy gets trapped in tight spaces

Building shapes are important

Chi flows easily round curves

A 'cutting' edge facing you is not beneficial

RIGHT **The way we arrange our cities and homes determines how chi energy moves. The design and structure of buildings are very important influences on our lifestyles and attitudes.**

TUNING INTO CHI

Energy is not a vague, unidentifiable happening – it has real impact. It makes its mark and is there for everyone to read. Getting information about chi energy is simply a matter of learning to ask the right questions.

Every time we use the word 'chi', we are talking about energy specifically in the way it moves through our world as a motivating force. We can describe the energy, or chi, of a room (or a place, an object or even a person) by talking in terms of colours or feelings or shapes. By trying to describe the energy in this way, we can attempt to gain a more accurate understanding of it. For example, we could describe a space and its energy by saying:

"It's got a kind of morning feel to it."

"It's a very lively place where lots of people get together for a good time, like a perpetual summer holiday."

"It's very self-contained; it would be easy for me to concentrate on any task there."

"It's not the sort of place where I could stay for long; it's very abrasive and bright; the energy's too high, all sharp angles and bright colours. Certainly no place to sleep, but maybe good for getting an idea for a project."

Making lists of observations about places and how colours, shapes, times and spaces affect the environment and combine to create certain types of chi can help us to map all of this information. We can use the information to make sense of our surroundings and create the spaces that we need.

Fortunately, earlier Feng Shui practitioners have already done a huge amount of the mapping for us, and at a time in history when the complications of modern living were not there to create a barrier between ourselves and a proper awareness of nature and the movement of chi.

In the art of Feng Shui, we have at our disposal a charting of the chi that so intimately and profoundly affects our lives. It remains for us to keep this body of knowledge alive and growing.

YIN AND YANG

Yin and Yang are another Chinese concept fundamental to Feng Shui. Broadly speaking, Yin and Yang are a way of describing forces at work in the world. Yin and Yang are opposing energies, present in all things in life; some things are predominantly Yin, and some are more Yang. Everything is relative and constantly changing.

Yin and Yang are as two parts of a whole. Yang rains down from the heavens, contracting, heating, gaining direction and purpose as it moves towards the open cup of Yin's acceptance from deep within the earth. At its most extreme moment, the thrust and gathered passion of Yang's creative force is given space to manifest itself by the deep, dark and cool reception of an all-nurturing, all-allowing Yin energy. Yin opens to yield a movement of rising growth, which disperses upwards to be reunited at its moment of broadest pause with the Heaven's force. Thus at its extreme it returns to Yang.

Another ancient Chinese way of describing natural energies in the world is the system of the five elements, or five transformations. The elements are earth, fire, water, wood and metal, and each has various associations and affinities.

ABOVE **The Yin-Yang symbol shows the balance in all things. Yin is receptive, cold and soft, while Yang is active, hot and compact. It is important to create a balance between these two forces.**

BELOW **Yin is perceived as the open cup that receives the downward force of Yang energy. The Chinese perceive Yin as a 'feminine' energy and Yang as a 'masculine' energy.**

ABOVE **According to Feng Shui principles, a well-ordered kitchen is the heart of a healthy home, but it is also important to get the** correct balance of the elements. It is usually best to avoid mixing fire and water, so the sink should be sited away from the cooker.

Enlightenment; action; highly visible; happening now; midday; midsummer; flame colours/ red; triangular.

Resourceful; centred; nurturing; rhythmical; balance; afternoon; late summer as it turns to autumn; times of transition; yellow; square.

Growth; new beginnings and ideas; rising upwards; breaking new ground; rapid movement; input; morning; spring; green; rectangular.

Complete; consolidated; ordered; structured; stylized; quintessential; pure; joy; evening; autumn; white; gold; silver; round.

Power within; contemplative interior; inactive exterior; dormancy; midnight; midwinter; blue/black; irregular/flowing.

ABOVE **The five elements symbolize certain actions, conditions of mind and seasons of the year.**

FIRE · EARTH · WOOD · METAL · WATER

CULTIVATING CHI

Once we have learnt how to identify with a space and think about the quality of chi there, many things become possible. We can ask ourselves, for instance, whether it is a predominantly Yin or Yang space. If it is a cool, quiet place where you can feel safe and nurtured, somewhere to retreat to at the end of the day, it is a Yin space, especially if it feels open and sprawling, maybe irregularly shaped with low level furnishings and soft contours. If it is a predominantly Yang space, it will be a place for clear thought and direct action, a space that will help you to get things done, where you can organize yourself and increase your concentration. It may be a tight, upright space, perhaps a narrow room with high windows and bare floors.

FAR RIGHT **The kind of office space people work in can have a direct bearing upon their ability to think clearly and act efficiently. A predominantly Yang space will help clear, quick thinking and decision-making.**

ABOVE **If you are planning a lively get-together with friends, it's a good idea to choose a predominantly Yang** **setting for it. Yang features in the room will enliven the conversation and stimulate the atmosphere.**

GETTING THE PICTURE

Asking yourself direct questions about shapes, functions and the capabilities of a space will give very specific answers about the energy quality and the Yin/Yang balance. Get as complete a picture as possible, working through a list of observations about overall room shape, ceiling height, window location and type. Look at window frames and other joinery in the room such as skirting boards and doors. Then look at the wall, floor and window coverings, furniture type and placement and all other contents and decoration. Think also in terms of acoustics – how the room sounds. A Yang room will sound clear and bright, a Yin room will be muffled and muted.

THE RIGHT MIX

Once we have identified the Yin and Yang features, we can decide if the room is predominately Yin or Yang and assess the space for its possible function and potential. If it is a very Yin space, it will be more suited to a Yin activity such as sleeping or reading a book, than a Yang activity such as a lively meeting. On the other hand, if it is a very Yang space, it will be more suitable for a Yang function, such as a children's playroom or home office, than a Yin activity such as enjoying a massage or watching an artistic film.

Learning to get the balance right in terms of creating more Yin spaces for Yin activities, and more Yang spaces for Yang activities, is a good starting point for anyone beginning to work with chi.

YANG

action; angles; closeness; narrow shapes; clarity and precision of style; shiny and compound surfaces; dense materials; bright shapes and colours; easily accessible spaces; long straight corridors, easy exits.

YIN

nurturing; soft, curvy shapes; sensuous fabrics in muted colours; low furnishings; sprawling layouts; hidden details; comfort and items to encourage relaxation; layers of floor and window coverings; safety.

LEFT **The combination of Yin and Yang colours and shapes in this bedroom will enliven it and boost the energy levels of the occupant, making her feel refreshed and lively after a night's sleep, as well as encouraging optimism and a cheerful outlook on life.**

RIGHT **The relaxing shades of blue in this predominantly Yin bedroom will promote a feeling of peace and tranquillity. This is an ideal retreat from the world. However, avoid putting a rug on the wall, choose a tapestry instead.**

RIGHT **This Yang bathroom, with its shiny surfaces and vibrant colours, will boost people's energy levels.**

BELOW **This angular glass vase is a good example of a Yang decorative object.**

LEFT **Yin fabrics will be soft, with muted colours; Yang fabrics will be brightly coloured.**

BELOW **Although this sofa seems to invite relaxation, the orange tones are Yang and will be stimulating rather than restful.**

A MATTER OF BALANCE

There is no such thing as a totally Yin or a totally Yang space: the energies tend to move towards or away from each other. If you try to create the most Yang environment possible in the hope that it will motivate your partner to do her accounts, you may find she becomes so energized that she rushes off to pack a bag to go to China, or she may simply overload and turn from Yang to Yin and fall asleep. So – create a sense of balance in your environment.

1

grasping the basics

TOP 10 QUESTIONS

寧握基礎

Which areas of my life can Feng Shui help?

Practising Feng Shui is like using holistic medicine: the entirety of a situation is addressed, with everything seen as a part of the whole. You can work on key issues, of course, but the long-term aim is to create overall balance and harmony.

Will what I do affect just me or everybody who uses the space?

It will make a difference to everyone who lives in the space, including any animals. The adjustments you make will also affect guests and visitors, but to a lesser extent.

How long will it be before I begin to get results?

I have seen Feng Shui have immediate and dramatic effects, but it can also take time. Possibly the process is connected to our ability to adapt to change. Feng Shui can help you get the most from your life, but just as glowing good health needs careful attention to diet, exercise and lifestyle, Feng Shui will require a little time and care before you see dramatic results.

Should I try to sort out all the Feng Shui in the home at once, or should I aim to do it gradually, a room at a time?

Start by doing a room at a time, and start with the one that most concerns you. If you want to focus on energy levels for instance, tackle your bedroom first. If your career is your priority, then look at your hall (see page 125).

宇
握
基
礎

We live in a very tall town house. Is it a Yin or Yang property? What would it be suitable for?

It sounds like a Yang house, and would suit an ambitious family or couple who want to get on in life. You can achieve things here, but you will have to work hard. It will not be restful.

Could I make Feng Shui mistakes that would produce major problems for my home and family?

No, as long as you trust your instinct and always monitor the effects of the changes you make. For example, before redecorating a room in a new colour, try introducing some accessories in that colour first and see how they contribute to the energy of the room.

I need to create a workspace in my bedroom. Will this mess up the Yin/Yang energy?

It will alter the energy and the Yin/Yang balance, making the bedroom more Yang and active. Aim to keep your work and leisure activities separate, and arrange the room so that you cannot see the workspace from the bed.

Are there some spaces that are equally Yin and Yang, or wholly Yin or Yang?

No. There will always be an emphasis of one quality over the other, and there will always be some Yin within a Yang space, and some Yang within Yin. This is shown in the Yin/Yang symbol (*see page 13*), which reflects constant movement and balance between Yin and Yang within a perfect whole.

Can Feng Shui help people who do not believe in it?

I have seen some immediate and powerful effects rewarding the work of self-confessed unbelievers. Feng Shui is not a form of mysticism or magic, it works directly with the chi or energy of a space, and will have an effect whether or not people can feel it or know that it is being used.

How will I know if the Feng Shui is working?

Things will start to change. They may happen on a subtle level, for example your happiness may increase or your attitude to life may alter. Things may also happen in a more tangible way, such as an unexpected phone call with a job offer, or an invitation to a party.

2
redirecting your chi

Whenever I carry out a Feng Shui consultation, the first thing I do is to spend at least an hour listening to the client, in order to get a real understanding of what life is like for him or her, and for other people who live or work in the particular space. My immediate reading of the client's chi will affect the whole course of the consultation, from initial diagnosis through to any remedies that might be suggested. Information will be constantly checked and reassessed during the course of the consultation and in any subsequent work. I will usually ask a client where he or she would like to be for our first talk. The chosen spot may be in the kitchen over a cup of tea, or the quiet of a more formal sitting room, or even the garden. Everything, from the choice of location to the way we are positioned in that space, and the way things are placed around us, will provide the kind of information needed to assess the work to be done.

The client may already have begun to make changes, using Feng Shui awareness of the space. This usually happens because, at the time of booking a consultation, a person's awareness of space is heightened in anticipation of my arrival, and he or she is inspired to make alterations. Clutter may have been noticed and cleared, things may have been rearranged, or decisions made about what does and does not work. So by the time I arrive, Feng Shui may already be very much in action, and chi on the move.

Some people may wonder about all this 'people watching'. After all, isn't Feng Shui about spaces and places, not people? In the broadest possible terms, Feng Shui involves finding the right space and arrangement of that space for any individual, group or company at any one time. In order to do this, it is necessary to observe people and their needs in detail before making recommendations, because each individual will have different requirements. However, because the very nature of life is change, it will always be necessary to review Feng Shui arrangements on an ongoing basis, to take into account any changes that come into our lives.

FAR LEFT **A Feng Shui practitioner will first listen to the person who is asking for advice, noting any personal habits, needs and attitudes before suggesting alterations. All of these factors give clues about where energy is moving or may be blocked.**

FENG SHUI IN ACTION

There is no such thing as a bad space. Every space will have something to offer someone at some time, for some purpose. However, a space that is ideal for a family, for example, could prove too challenging for an elderly couple, and a space suited to a highly motivated career woman may need some adjustments when she decides that she wants to have a family.

On a more subtle level, a man who calls in a Feng Shui consultant to help improve his job prospects may be discovered to be so lacking in self-confidence that he has made himself virtually invisible in the workplace. Feng Shui may help a couple to feel nurtured and safe in their home, fuelling their ability to succeed in the world, but this new-found independence may perhaps also cause them to drift apart.

Asking the right questions, giving someone the time and support to answer in a valuable way, and listening to the way the person answers are important. Try answering the list of questions below.

RIGHT **This workspace has a good blend of Yin and Yang aspects. In this context, the rounded sofas are Yin, while the sharp angles of the computer machinery on the desk are Yang. Muted colours contrasted with bright orange tones also blend Yin and Yang energies.**

ASKING THE RIGHT QUESTIONS

A Feng Shui practitioner will want to know:

■ How did you come to be living/working here?

■ Where did you live/work before, and what are the main differences or similarities between the two places?

■ What happened and how did you feel when you first saw your new home/workspace? How easily was the move negotiated?

■ What did you initially envisage doing with the space?

■ Have you put any of your earlier plans into practice and, if so, how have they worked for you?

■ What has happened in life since you have lived/worked here?

■ What do you know about the history of the space? Why did the previous occupants move on?

■ What do you want out of the space? What would you like to achieve or have happen while you are here?

■ What are the positive things about this space?

■ What are the negative things about this space?

■ Are you happy to stay in this space?

If you have run through this list of questions by yourself or with a friend, you may have unearthed some surprising details about your relationship to your space. For example, your decision to be in the space at all (or apparent lack of control over the event) may have come from less than positive motives.

Life may have altered radically since the move in a way you did not expect, or it may not have altered in the way you had hoped. Alternatively, you may have revealed what a wonderful space you are in, how well everything has gone from the move, and the happy times that you have spent there. However, the challenge in this case may be that guests love the chi in your home so much that they never want to leave. Either way, you have begun to practise Feng Shui and understand more about the pattern of your life.

FRESH INSIGHT

Look back over your answers to the questions. Could you equally well have been talking about things other than your space? Your partner, your career, your life in general? Looking at your life, using your space as a reflection of it will give you fresh ideas. It can help your understanding of yourself and give practical solutions to seemingly insurmountable problems.

We are now going to look at five types of chi (associated with the five elements) that are present in us, and in our environments, in varying proportions. The challenge is to get the balance right, at any one time, between the chi of the space and the chi of the occupants.

ABOVE **This figure represents the fire element – hot, expansive energy. Fire stimulates conversation and lively entertainment, and is the force that expresses activity. The colour red is associated with this element, and will boost energy levels.**

HIGHLY ACTIVE CHI – FIRE

In a house where fire is the controlling element, there will usually be something 'happening'. Walk up the bright, open path and through the wide open door, and the sound of laughter, perhaps even song, may strike you. Even on a quiet day it will seem as though something is just about to happen. In a room along the corridor someone could be making a film, in the kitchen a lunch party may be in full swing, and it would be no surprise to find a heated conversation in the dining room being led by an animated couple dressed in red.

Extreme? Yes. This is a place of extremes and heightened activity. While you live here, whatever you do here will absorb you totally and be the talk of the town.

Fire energy is Yang at its most extreme, the 'high summer' of places to be. Its features include triangular building plots with a southerly aspect, tall buildings on smallish plots, long thin gardens with straight paths, red bricks, triangular roofs, and red roof tiles.

The interior of such a home will be light, perhaps too bright, with very angular features and many shiny surfaces.

Does it wear you out just thinking about it? Or is it just where you would like to be, as a visitor? A predominantly fire type of environment can be a wonderful place to visit, but if it is not balanced with other elements it could 'burn out'.

BELOW **This well-lit room is dominated by fire. It has a sloping ceiling, shiny surfaces and objects, and a lot of red hues. Too much fire can cause arguments to break out, or even fights.**

THE FIVE ELEMENTS

Element	Colour range	Compass direction	Activity
Water	Blue Navy blue Black	North	Contemplation Quiet Deep power Sexuality
Wood	Green	East	Growth Development New ideas Planning
Fire	Red Flame colours	South	Action Enlightenment Self-esteem Public status
Earth	Yellow Natural earth colours	Centre	Relationships Nurturing Ability to be centred Resourcefulness
Metal	White Silver Gold	West	Order Structure Leisure and pleasure Creativity

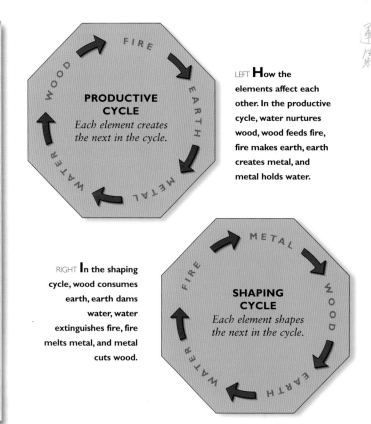

LEFT **H**ow the elements affect each other. In the productive cycle, water nurtures wood, wood feeds fire, fire makes earth, earth creates metal, and metal holds water.

RIGHT **I**n the shaping cycle, wood consumes earth, earth dams water, water extinguishes fire, fire melts metal, and metal cuts wood.

TURNING DOWN THE HEAT

There are a number of things we can do to reduce an excess of fire energy. For example, imagine planning a party in a south-facing room (the direction of fire is south) that has other distinctly 'fire' features, such as a sloping ceiling and a red carpet; in the centre of the room is a glass table with some tiger lilies on it. This room will create so much activity that arguments, perhaps even a fight, are likely to break out amongst its occupants.

We could reduce the level of fire energy by taking away some of the fiery items. We could remove the flowers and the table, for instance, or we could balance them by introducing another element to absorb some of the fire energy. For example, we could add some earth energy by covering the table with a yellow cloth. The yellow cloth will absorb some of the fire because fire creates earth (for a full list of the elements and how they feed or control each other, see the charts above). It would be a mistake to swap the glass (fire) table for a rectangular wooden one, however, because wood feeds fire. If we could change the red carpet, that would be really effective and the addition of a soft, earth-coloured fabric at the window to cut the glare would also help. It would also be advisable to move guests on to another room once a party has got going, if possible.

Appropriate occasions for spending time in a fire-dominated room would include, for example, times when a person's self-esteem is at a low ebb, or bright insights are needed into a particular problem. However, if you find that too much activity, stress and sudden mood swings happen regularly in your life, then you should aim to reduce the levels of fire chi in your space. You should also try to reduce any wood items that may be feeding the fire energy.

RIGHT **The element of water brings a sense of calm and stillness to our surroundings. A water-dominated environment will help any activities that require contemplation. Water features include softened textures, muted colours and rounded curves, and hidden spaces.**

CONTEMPLATION – WATER

To sense the essence of the water element, imagine a house, far from the road in a hidden spot, where stillness and the quiet of midnight reign. As you stand and wait to make your presence known, no lights flicker on. Walk in through the open door and pause again to look round the dimly lit bowl-shaped entrance hall before moving quietly through a series of open rooms.

Here is a place to sit and rest, to have silent conversations with yourself and to restore your body and soul. Although the atmosphere may appear to be passive, all around there is a feeling that work has just been completed. This could be the house of a poet, healer or great thinker. It is the kind of space that can support us while we work deep into the night, and will allow us the flexibility to survive a period of removal from the world at large. There is nothing to jar or excite; everything is possible in this building, even though at first glance it may appear that nothing is happening.

A CALM RETREAT

A typical water-dominated home could be a north-facing, rambling cottage with low ceilings, and windows slightly obscured with curtains or plants. It could also be a low, sprawling winter cabin. It is a home to get lost in, with unexpected doorways leading to secret rooms, perhaps with a seat by a window that invites a dreamy afternoon's contemplation. Here colours flow and swirl, textures absorb and angles bend. Expect a room with velvet drapes; a bedroom so blue it feels like a pool; a study where a writing table gives way to an easy chair pulled up by a window with a view. An artist may have painted frescos on the walls or a poet inscribed a verse above the door, and the only candles to be found float in a water lily bowl.

At this extreme, it is the perfect place for an expectant mother to labour towards the birth of her child, a weary business person to rest and recuperate, or an artist to wander in to gain inspiration. As long as we do not overdo it, we all need some water energy in our environment, especially as life becomes busier and more frantic.

ABOVE **These candles floating in a bowl of water combine water and fire, as well as Yin and Yang. The candles will add a spark of energy to the reflectiveness produced by the rounded bowl and the water within.**

ABOVE **Lighting a fire will enliven a water-dominated home and add a sense of purpose to contemplation.**

ABOVE **The fire of this angled, glass vase and red flowers will be softened by the water at the bottom.**

ABOVE **The wood and earth energy of this picture will help to balance an excess of water in a room.**

INTRODUCING CALM ENERGY

To acknowledge the need to dream and be still is essential, and it is easy to achieve with placement and design. To create a sense of tranquillity, go for curving walls and corridors. Archways, arched windows, angles softened with fabric or paint effects, the introduction of soft blues or even a hint of black, will all make surroundings less abrasive and more relaxing. Place a comfortable chair in a quiet spot, giving yourself a place to be calm, and the relaxation will follow. This is the essence of Feng Shui: creating space that allows you to do the things that you need to do.

STEMMING THE FLOW

There may be times when we need to add some energy to the calm of a water-dominated place, such as during the final stages of labour, or to help recovery from fatigue. Both of these require an upward turn in energy. We can achieve this by adding a little of the wood element to the environment. Wood energy represents organization and planning. And if we are not to become too self-absorbed and introspective, perhaps too gloomy and cold, we need a little fire, and then some earth to settle and centre us. And what balance is there to be had without the order and structure of metal energy?

So, to prevent an over-dominance of the water element, it is easy to make small adjustments to the space, which will insert other elements to balance the effects of water. We could walk through this 'water wonderland', opening doors and pulling back blinds. We could hang a series of framed pictures high up on a wall, remove the cosy cushions from the easy chair, roll up the carpet, and light a fire. We could add splashes of turquoise and green, buy some tulips and arrange them in a clear glass vase, and then we would have included enough of the other elements (see page 21) to have achieved a real sense of balance.

We create spaces that are reflections of ourselves but, unfortunately, these may reflect our own imbalances, and then we become stuck in a spiral circling into ever more imbalance. I once did a consultation at a house without a single place to sit anywhere, even in the room where the family ate their meals. The family found that things were going wrong for them. They had tried changing their diets and researched all kinds of alternative lifestyles and healthcare, but the harder they worked to solve their problems, changing first this and then that, the worse things became for them. The first step to a solution to their problems lay in something as simple as rearranging the five elements in their home, and its contents. This is Feng Shui in action in all its wonderful simplicity.

RIGHT **When metal is in harmony with the other four elements, a sense of order and clarity is produced, but too much metal in an environment can deplete energy and give rise to gloom.**

ABOVE **The simplicity of this clutter-free, all-white room gives a sense of release and freedom, and enables clear thought, precise action and completion of tasks.**

STRUCTURE AND STYLE – METAL

Sometimes following fashions in interior design can cause the elements to get out of balance and affect Feng Shui. I once worked on a space that was all white. A young graphic designer had painstakingly created a series of rooms where pure function, grace and beauty had reached the level of the sublime. The contents of the bedroom had been reduced to a white, shrouded bed, a simple metallic clothes rail that supported white or navy clothes, and a slim volume of poetry placed by the bed. The sitting room contained a sleek arrangement of artwork and gathered information, whilst the kitchen only revealed itself as such by the presence of a stainless steel sink and spotless white cooker. No unsightly food cluttered the pristine worktops or the single cupboard. It is very easy for this type of space to overbalance into the extreme.

Once embarked on the creation of a space of such clean lines of structure and function, we can get a little addicted to the sense of joy and release gained by letting go of so much we have identified as useless. However, the clarity and sense of order this brings can clear the way for us to see the underlying structure of our surroundings and our lives. It then becomes possible to identify connections with meaningful people and events, communication becomes a pleasure, and creativity flows easily.

METAL ENERGY IN BALANCE

Metal energy in perfect harmony with the other elements plays its part as life's great harvester. In this type of environment, all that we have sown we are able to reap. A home with balanced metal energy will be tidy, clean and in good order. Rooms are easy to move around in and use, decorations are clear-cut and uncluttered. The whole space is well lit and well ordered. Each area echoes and adds to the one before, and the whole building functions in an easy, streamlined fashion. Nowhere does a colour jar or a misplaced object intrude upon the occupants' creative flow.

In this home, if you need something it will be there, just as you hoped and expected. Nothing unnecessary will clutter your thoughts. Perhaps a vase of white lilies wafts a beautiful aroma through the clear, wide halls, which are the airways and lungs of the house.

ABOVE **Neatly-folded objects, such as these towels, echo the order that metal brings.**

ABOVE **Soften an excess of metal by adding contrasting cushions to a white sofa or chairs.**

ABOVE **Curved accessories moderate metal's cutting edge. This cup will bring water energy too.**

LEFT **The metal energy in this bathroom is increased by the terracotta floor, because earth energy nourishes metal. This bathroom also contains wood and water chi. The triangular shape made by the curtains creates fire energy.**

Particular attention will have been paid to keeping entrances and exits clear. The attic will probably contain only a simple, uncluttered chest, and a family of protected (and rather rare) bats.

Visit this home and you will leave with your mind clear, your intuition charged and a firm idea for your latest creative project – and just how to communicate all your new insights to your partner.

SOFTENING UP

Order, clarity and joy are the result when metal is in harmony with the other elements, but depletion, brittleness and gloom arise when it has become extreme. The perfect circle of metal energy's expression can only benefit from the addition of the gentle curve of water energy. The softening of a line, the addition of a little depth to what can otherwise become excessively two-dimensional, can moderate the cutting edge of metal.

Brittle metal energy also needs nourishing with a little earth chi, so that it can once more brim and flow into water. So, in the unbalanced metal environment of the graphic designer mentioned earlier, you would look to earth and water chi to find your remedies. Warm up some of that white with sunny, earthy colours. Soften some of the precise lines of the kitchen with the addition of a place to sit and eat. Then add somewhere to prepare and cook the food that will have appeared around the kitchen.

If the windows in a room with too much metal element open to the west, soften their lines by using a fabric with a texture so sensuous that you have to stop and enjoy it every time you pass. Layer the walls with paper, paint and adornment, and add riches and resonance to the crystalline sparkle that has made everything a little too stark and bare. Introduce humorous touches to the decor, particularly in the bathroom, and add warmer colours to pale rooms by including some gently coloured towels, bed linen, cushions or crockery.

The idea is not to intrude on this sensitively aligned space with masses of loud colours, but to allow the chi to move by adding soft, flowing water energy, and supportive earth energy.

RIGHT **People who have a lot of wood energy around them usually start a lot of new projects. However, if there is an excess of wood chi in your environment, you may become irritated by being unable to find time to complete jobs that you have started.**

UPRIGHT ENERGY – WOOD

Imagine a meeting is about to begin. It is early morning and everything has been ready since dawn. The long, rectangular table is polished, and high-backed chairs await their occupants. In the surrounding rooms a family prepares for the new day. All the children have busy schedules and are prepared to work hard. Windows, and a main door to the east, flood morning light into the room.

This is wood energy in balance. These people know where they are going and intend to get there. Wood energy gives us the ability to break new ground, but sometimes it does it in a shocking and potentially disruptive and unstable way.

Wood interiors are often innovative and fashionable, and living in them can feel like being part of an ongoing project or reconstruction. The interiors are full of ideas and newness, perhaps looking a little too freshly scrubbed, but with heartening touches of beauty that are positioned ready for purposeful use.

Remember, however, that it is very easy for this energy to become unstable because of the high standards needed to achieve desired goals. Listen for the first raised voice; watch for the first crack to appear in the paintwork. Too many projects begun, and too much purpose and forethought in the layout and design, signal imbalance in this chi. This is a very upright energy, and attracts the eye ever upwards and ever forwards.

ABOVE **This upright, wooden stand symbolizes wood's rising energy.**

Uplighters provide wood energy

Tall cabinets

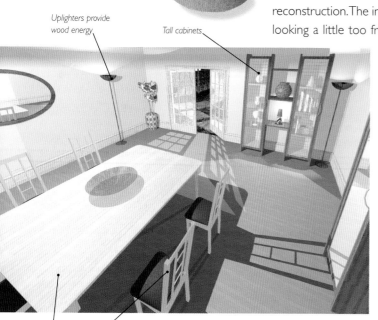

High-backed chairs

Rectangular table

ABOVE **This is a wood-dominated room, with its tall cabinets, upright chairs, rectangular table, wooden floor and uplighters. The touches of blue add water chi, so feeding the wood.**

INCREASING WOOD CHI

If you find that you lack the ability to think ahead or start new projects, or if you rarely feel wonder and delight at the sheer business of being alive, you could boost your chi with a few changes in your environment. Think about the purpose of each room and tailor the contents accordingly. Arrange decor to take your attention upwards, even going so far as to move door handles or lighting, if necessary. Uplighting, especially, will boost wood energy. Ideally pictures should depict positive, outdoor scenes – hang them

ABOVE **Uplighters are features of the wood element, because they draw the eye upwards in accordance with wood's upward drive.**

a little higher than usual. Introduce some upright furnishings, perhaps a high table with a vase of spring blossoms. Keep window coverings light, and position them to the sides of the windows. Introduce a clean, fresh look to halls and passageways. Pay special attention to bathrooms and any east- or north-facing rooms; remember that the water element is affected by energy from the north, and that it feeds wood (see page 21).

REDUCING WOOD ENERGY

If having fun and relaxation are difficult for you, or if you start too many projects and then cannot see them through, then you need to allow less wood energy to express itself in your environment.

Do this by taking a walk round your home, noting down all evidence of unfinished jobs and projects. Work thoroughly, starting with rooms designed for rest and relaxation, and complete as many of the outstanding tasks as you can. If this makes you irritable, light a real fire or a red candle and try again. Add some fiery and light-hearted objects to key rooms – they should be things without purpose or intent such as a beautiful vase of full-blown roses or a photograph showing someone you love having a really good time. Remove a few clocks and add touches of pink or peach wherever you can. Burn some rose oil in an oil burner (remember to add a few drops of the oil to some water in the oil reservoir) and let the heady scent fire your passion for life.

For the longer term, try to redecorate your space to reduce the amount of wood energy and add some more of the fire element (for appropriate colours see page 21). If you have wood-dominated seating in the sitting room, such as a high-backed, green sofa, try to change it, or add some orange or red cushions. You should also assess the quality of your entire space: if you have a garden, open it out, and cut down any tall trees. If you have a choice of bedrooms, move out of the top floor bedroom in favour of one nearer the ground, and hang any pictures slightly lower than usual.

When correcting an excess of wood energy, it is best to try remedies that can be put into place with little planning and effort, things that will involve action and fun. And getting a 'fiery' friend in to help you is often the best remedy of all.

BELOW **If you have an excess of wood chi, it may be difficult to relax. Red candles, pink, red or peach roses, and** **anything representing the fire element will enable you to unwind and enjoy an evening's entertainment.**

27

RIGHT **In Feng Shui,
earth provides a sense
of hearth and home. Its
colours are those of
the earth: brown,
amber, yellow,
terracotta and sand. It
is associated with
abundance and
resourcefulness.**

RESOURCE AND SOURCE – EARTH

To picture a balanced earth environment, imagine a place of great abundance and nurturing, where a certain stillness rests. Once you have walked through the door, a sense of having come home descends on you. There is a strength at the centre of this household, for even if it is the home of a sole occupant, there will be a great sense of 'home and hearth' here.

Life will proceed uninterrupted here, regardless of the inconsistencies and challenges that may disrupt life for the world beyond. In this place almost any amount of change or difficulty can be absorbed and transformed from adversity into gift. A broken vase turns quietly into a mosaic, stale bread becomes a pudding, an overwrought child is soon in the garden exercising a bored dog, and an angry teenager is set to chopping logs for a fire that will warm the bones of an ageing aunt. Everyone is provided for, everything is put to a good purpose.

As summer turns to autumn, the great transitional, balancing power of earth energy gears the transformation from fire to earth. At the centre of this balanced earth environment you will find a place that is uncluttered, peaceful and safe.

Walk to the south-west and glowing amber and yellow is likely to adorn rooms and hallways. This is a home where everyone usually ends up in the warm and lively kitchen, lending a hand to peel vegetables for the never-ending soup, chatting whilst pastry is rolled out on a wide table, or stirring the sauce while a child's knee is cleaned and bandaged. Evidence of ongoing practical action is all over the house. Washing is folded and stacked on its way to be ironed, a basket full of cut blooms and a pair of gardening gloves are in the conservatory, and a pile of letters ready to be sent is on a table in the hall. Even the floors echo the earth energy in this place. In the hall, a deep rug adorns a polished wood floor, and in the conservatory the floor is a wonderful mosaic. The sitting room harbours a sandy coloured carpet, and the kitchen has a floor covered in old terracotta tiles.

ABOVE **When earth
chi is in balance,
everything is put to
good use. (A kitchen is
usually its active heart.)
Ongoing practical
action will be especially
evident here.**

ABOVE **This basket of
fruit and vegetables
typifies the abundance
to be found in an earth-
dominated home.**

ABOVE **Square, earth-
coloured cushions will
contribute earth
energy to a living room
or bedroom.**

ABOVE **Square, gilt-
framed mirrors will
also add earth chi to
your home, and add a
sense of stability.**

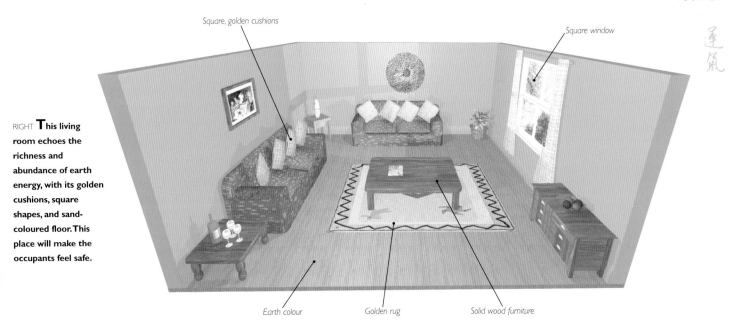

Square, golden cushions

Square window

RIGHT **This living room echoes the richness and abundance of earth energy, with its golden cushions, square shapes, and sand-coloured floor. This place will make the occupants feel safe.**

Earth colour

Golden rug

Solid wood furniture

EARTH ENERGY IN BALANCE

Earth energy enables us to utilize all available resources and put everything to good use. To boost earth energy, clear out that central hallway or room and clarify its function before replacing its furniture and contents – in this way you will create a powerful, balanced and free-flowing space. Position your rubbish bin with as much care as your cooker and bed. Clean your toilet with as much love as you cleanse your skin. Acknowledge the whole, and the interdependence of all parts, of your home.

LACK OF EARTH ENERGY

Depleted earth chi will produce a place bereft of that warm glow of rhythm, shelter and safe progress. This space will not feel like home to the occupants. Look first to the kitchen, where there will be an absence of places to cook or prepare food and nowhere to store 'real' food. Too many sharp, hard surfaces, or too many windows and doors, dissipate chi and bounce it around when it needs to be slowing down and accumulating.

In the dining room, cool, watery colours and high-backed chairs may intimidate guests and make them nervous. Add some earth energy by introducing sunshine tones, and place a large square rug under the table. Put square, not round, cushions on the chairs. If there is a dead-end passage, put a mirror at the end. Fix any doors that will not open easily. If you are short of storage space, get some cupboards built. Now look at the south-west part of the house. Are there piles of clutter or neglected rooms? Clear the clutter, clean everywhere thoroughly, then put those rooms to good use to recreate the natural rhythm of the home.

EARTH OVERLOAD

When an excess of earth energy is present, there will be cupboards stuffed with so-called 'useful things', too many activities in progress, and too many furnishings and objects, particularly items inherited from other people. No house can, or should be, all things. Trying to make a lobby into a music room, or a corner into a place to store arts and crafts materials, may send the whole thing into overload.

Remedy an excess of earth energy by adding the structure of metal. Clear any clutter, identify key activities and priorities and reduce the rest. Take colours back from bright yellows to pale creams, or wash the walls with paler whites.

2 redirecting your chi

TOP 10 QUESTIONS

I need more wood energy in my home, but my ceilings are very low and the windows are small. What else can I do to bring in more of the wood element?

Add the colour green and bring in more organized space, because wood energy represents organization and planning. You could also hang pictures and mirrors higher up the walls.

My career seems to have gone off-track since I moved into my present home. Should I move?

Your career going off-track is signalling a change that you need to make. You may have an altered perspective or different aims now. If your move was out of choice, you don't need to move again. Just work with the changes in your life.

Once I have identified a problem, how will I know how to solve it?

Correct and timely identification of the cause of a problem is a major step towards solving it. We are not working to speed up energy or bounce it around with mirrors and bells. We are trying to allow a space to find its own power and balance, so once the first cause of a problem is found, the remedy will also become apparent.

My husband has lost his energy and interest in life. We share the same bedroom, yet my energy is fine. What could be causing it?

What suits one person may not suit another. Look at the room from his viewpoint: there may be a heavy item of furniture near his side of the bed, or some cutting chi. Try to identify the cause and change it.

We always seem to have arguments in our kitchen. Why?

Kitchens are often where arguments happen. They frequently have sharp angles and shiny, abrasive surfaces, with water and fire too near each other. Put a plant between the sink and the cooker, a cloth over the table, and soften any harsh lines and edges.

Is it best to get a mixture of all five elements in every room?

Yes, every room needs all the elements, but each room will need a predominance of one element. Balance rather than mixture is the key. Refer to the productive and shaping cycles on page 21, then plan each room and its accessories.

Is it possible to work on my own space, or would it be better to ask someone less involved to do it?

You can work on your own space, but it helps if you can look at it with detachment, as an outsider would. A good time to do this is after you have spent a few days on holiday away from your home. Alternatively, ask a friend to help you.

I've been feeling tired for no reason recently. Is it due to a lack of fire energy?

Not necessarily. It is more likely to be the overall flow of chi in the house. Look for a change in your life around the time the fatigue started, then work through this book to find a possible cause. Also look to your diet.

How can I create a space that will help everyone living in it?

We are all living with certain people for specific reasons, and whatever we create in our lives and homes will affect them too. As you make changes, you will be able to learn a lot by the other occupants' reactions, and work through the issues that arise from them. This should help to improve the chi in your home.

How can working with the elements help me improve my finances?

Boosting metal energy in your home (see pages 24–5) will help you reap the rewards of your hard work. Look at your home and workspace: add structure and clarity, and clear any clutter. These measures should all help to improve your financial situation.

3
feng shui outside the home

屋外之風水

Until now all the Feng Shui we have been practising has kept us firmly inside our homes. However, we can also extend the connections to take in the space that exists beyond the front door.

THE VIEW FROM AFAR

If we compare the climates of North Africa and Scandinavia, it is easy to see that the hot African climate will enforce a very different lifestyle to that offered by the cooler climate of Scandinavia, and that each region will have different types of chi. The quality and balance of chi differ naturally around the world. The landscape chart on this page suggests which landscape features indicate the presence of a particular element. Use the guidelines in the chart as a way of fine-tuning your awareness about the area that surrounds and supports your home.

It is essential to look at a space in the context of its surroundings. Once we know which element predominates outside our home, we can make better choices when practising Feng Shui. However, trying to work on your home's Feng Shui while living in it is difficult, because you are too involved with your living space to view it with detachment. If we recall the people with the house with nowhere to sit down (see page 23), we can see that they did not recognize the problem. It was something they had created for themselves, and so much a part of their everyday reality that it had become normal. So we must find ways to increase our detachment from our space prior to practising Feng Shui, in order to apply it more effectively. Taking a holiday or break, far away from home, for at least four or five days, will help you to assess your home more clearly on your return.

ABOVE **W**hat effect does the area outside your home have on you? The landscape in the top picture will produce fire energy, whereas the tall buildings in the cityscape below have the upward thrust of rising wood energy.

FAR RIGHT **A** sprawling estate that displays some water element features will benefit from the fire and wood elements supplied by the high, red triangular roof on the central building. Living under it may confer a higher profile in the community!

FIVE ELEMENTS AND THE LANDSCAPE

Element	Shape	Landscape/architectural features
Water	Flowing, curving	Rambling, sprawling, flowing land and buildings
Wood	Rising upwards, rectangular	Tower blocks, high-rise developments, forests
Fire	Pointed, triangular	Pointed rooftops, mountains with peaks
Earth	Square, compact	Squat, box-shaped buildings, mountains with flat tops
Metal	Round, spherical	Dunes, hills, elliptical shapes, spherical buildings, round sweeps of land

ASSESSING OUR ENVIRONMENT

The first thing to do when making a reading of the area where we live, is to ask ourselves a series of general questions:

■ What sort of area is it?

■ What does the landscape look like?

■ What is the quality of the land?

■ Is it mountainous, hilly, flat or a valley?

■ Is it close to water and, if so, what type of water?

With the answers to these questions, we then need to translate the features we have observed into what we know about the five elements. For example, a city with plenty of tall, narrow buildings could be said to be the equivalent of a room full of upright furniture and high windows. The same could be said for an area planted with conifers or vegetation with a strong upward thrust, like bamboo. These features are indicative of the wood element, and denote rising wood energy.

An area of urban sprawl, with plenty of low-level housing in large estates along curving roads, is like a water-dominated house with hidden rooms. In this area there will be few people to direct you. Its rural equivalent will also be a fairly deserted place. This is a water environment, regardless of its proximity to actual water.

This raises an important and often overlooked point: the presence of lakes, rivers or streams, or other sources of water, does not necessarily denote a water element type of space. For example, an attractive fountain shooting water skywards could actually be expressing rising wood energy. It is the energetic qualities of the five elements that we need to understand, not necessarily their most obvious physical characteristics.

MAKING THE CONNECTION

Few of us will be able to find a single, obvious element in our surroundings; all places are a balance of the elements to a greater or lesser degree. Once you have identified some of the energetic qualities of your landscape, whether urban or rural, you can learn a lot from them and how they are affecting your home.

You should Refer to the productive and shaping cycles of elements *(see page 21)*; they will help you to assess the way your wider environment interacts with your home. If you have identified your landscape as a water space, for example, and your tall building with its series of pointed (triangular) red tiled roofs as a mixture of wood and fire, you will be able to see how the combination of these three elements will affect you and your neighbours. The community will probably benefit immensely from the existence of your house, with its fire and wood qualities. You too will be nurtured by your water environment, because water feeds wood, and wood feeds fire. You may also have found that, since moving to the house, you have a higher profile at work or in the community, and you may have more of a social life or an involvement in initiating and setting up leisure or sporting events as a result of the fire and wood energies.

The landscape chart opposite gives some guidelines for identifying the energies in different places, but it should not be used to squeeze the wonderful variety of urban and rural features into five types for the purpose of analysis. Instead, use the guidelines to hone your sensitivities to location. It would be better to try to understand, for example, the importance of stimulating active energy for people living in a remote valley.

Low-level housing

Houses randomly arranged

Curving path

Triangular, red roof

LEFT **The 'Mouth of Chi', the area of your main or front door, is where energy enters your home. The quality of this chi is greatly affected by the approach to your home, its appearance and surroundings.**

THE FRONT DOOR

The position of the front door is very important in Feng Shui practice, not only because of the direction it faces, but also because of what we find immediately beyond the door. Feng Shui is above all a study of energy, and the way chi flows through our lives. The quality of chi inside a building is directly related to the energy entering the building by way of its front, or main, door. This door is often called 'The Mouth of Chi' – a title that illustrates its role in feeding the environment with chi.

Nothing better illustrates Feng Shui in action than looking at how the placement of the front door works. The aim is to get your front door, or Mouth of Chi, supplied with the best 'food', or positive chi energy, that is possible.

THE APPROACH TO YOUR HOME

Here is an exercise that will help you to assess the nature of your own Mouth of Chi. Open the main door of your home, step out and close it behind you. You may want to take a notebook or tape recorder with you; taking notes often helps us to slow down and pay more attention.

Walk about a hundred metres (100 yards) away from your front door and then turn to approach as if for the first time. Be aware of everything that is happening around you. Notice sounds, sights, smells and feelings. If you know where the boundary line of your property starts, pay particular attention as you cross it. Is it well defined, marked by gates or an archway perhaps, or is it more low-key, delineated only by a change in the nature of the path?

The existence of obvious and well defined boundaries is of great significance in Feng Shui, and tells us a lot about the way we run our lives, and our concepts of the separation between 'self' and 'other'. Adding clearly marked boundaries to our space will help to add earth energy, which can be helpful if we are engaged in dealing with water energy personal issues, such as learning about our own inner power and how to use it, because earth controls water *(see page 21)*.

This exercise will help you to learn a great deal about the quality of chi available to your house and everyone who spends time there. It is important to carry out this process carefully, and trust your findings, so that you can ascertain exactly what you need to be doing in order to improve the Feng Shui of your home.

PHOENIX ENERGY

It is usually desirable to have a clear, open, beautiful space outside the main or front door of your home. This space is traditionally named 'The Bright Palace' or 'Phoenix' in Feng Shui terms. Phoenix chi represents the energy of the south and the fire element.

If possible, avoid having high brick walls at the front of your property, or looming conifers, tight alleyways, or thunderingly busy roads with traffic queuing daily. However, if a looming conifer is all that stands between you and the road, or an interestingly placed electricity pylon, think again about cutting the tree down and

ASSESSING THE MAIN ENTRANCE

As you approach your front door:
- What do you pass and where is it positioned (high, low, close by?)
- Imagine this is your first visit. What impression of the space would you be experiencing?
- How do you feel about entering the space?
- What do you expect to find inside, on the basis of the approach?
- Is it easy to arrive here?
- What sort of experience did you have doing this exercise?

ABOVE **These houses have good phoenix energy to the front, substantial tortoise chi** **at the back, and adequate tiger and dragon energy to the sides.**

give it a good feed with compost instead. Any structure that feels threatening to your space should be noted. Have a good look all around, high and low, near and far. Check for any sharp-angled edges of buildings or structures: they will have a negative effect on your home if they are pointing towards it. Sharp edges make the chi bounce off at an angle and create harmful energy known as 'poison arrows'. If you see any of these sharp edges pointing towards your home, you should consider placing some form of protection, such as a hedge, between your door and the structures in question in order to deflect the 'poison arrows', or negative energy.

A client of mine was concerned about a telegraph pole that was positioned directly outside her front door. Apart from this one obstruction, the phoenix energy of the home she had just bought after splitting up with her husband was completely clear, vibrant and wide open. When I asked her if she felt that there was anything preventing her moving forward in her new life, she answered that she felt extremely optimistic and clear-sighted, except for one obstruction – she had trouble seeing beyond her attachment to her ex-husband. The telegraph pole could be seen as a manifestation of this unwanted attachment to her ex-husband. It is very likely that, once she has moved past this obstacle in her life, the telephone company will eventually decide that the telegraph pole has become redundant and will remove it.

ABOVE **Keep your main door unobstructed so that positive chi can enter easily.**

ABOVE **The triangular shape created by this entrance will bring fire energy into your life.**

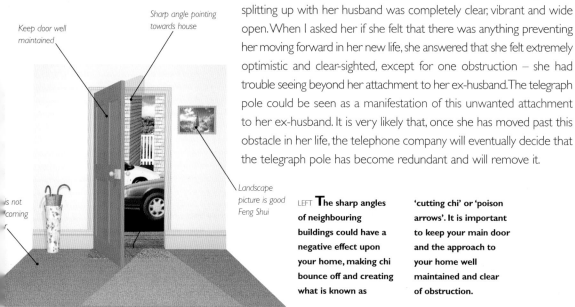

Keep door well maintained

Sharp angle pointing towards house

is not coming

Landscape picture is good Feng Shui

LEFT **The sharp angles of neighbouring buildings could have a negative effect upon your home, making chi bounce off and creating what is known as** **'cutting chi' or 'poison arrows'. It is important to keep your main door and the approach to your home well maintained and clear of obstruction.**

ABOVE **The white, stylised grandeur of this entrance expresses the energy of metal.**

35

DRAGON ENERGY

Dragon chi can be found to the left-hand side of the home when we are standing with the tortoise chi *(the energy at the rear of a building, see page 38)* behind us and the phoenix chi in front of us. It represents the energy of the east and the element wood. It should form a protective and supportive energy at the side of your home without overpowering it. Mythically, the dragon's wisdom and power comes from its mental prowess and the stabilizing energy of the earth. The dragon can move from beneath the ground to fly amongst the clouds, representing the scope of its power and the unique gift it gives to a space. Traditionally, Feng Shui practitioners would want to see a hill or a mound in this area. In an urban situation, a building would be substituted for this expression of dragon energy.

BELOW **A house should be built in a place where chi moves freely. Behind this house, hills provide comforting tortoise energy, but at the front of it the shrubs may obstruct phoenix energy. However, the shrubs may protect the house against negative chi.**

TIGER ENERGY

The tiger chi of a home is situated in the opposite position to dragon chi: when we are standing with tortoise chi behind us, and phoenix chi in front of us, it is on the right. The tiger represents the energy of the west and the element metal. Its action is likened to the pounce of a tiger, when a huge burst of gathered energy is suddenly released. The tiger usually appears as a land formation or some sort of building, which is smaller than that of the dragon, less solid than that of the tortoise, and of a more volatile, energetic nature.

SNAKE ENERGY

In the centre of your home lies the coiled power of the snake. Able to react instantly to stimuli from its environment, the snake represents stillness yet also implies movement, both of which we hope to find in a space. At the centre of a space there should be calm and clarity, because chaos here can hamper the smooth running of the whole space. This animal represents the element earth and the central axis around which all else revolves.

DRAGON ENERGY

Dragon chi is situated to the left of a building. A hill, large house or another big property to the left of your home will serve as its dragon chi. This provides your home with support and protection. Dragon energy is related to the east and the element wood.

PHOENIX ENERGY

Phoenix chi is found at the front of a building. Its upwardly-moving energy is linked to the south and it represents the element fire.

TIGER ENERGY

Tiger chi is on the right of a building. Like dragon chi, tiger chi may appear in the shape of a building or land formation (although smaller than that of the dragon), but is more volatile and energetic. Tiger chi represents the west and the element metal.

RIGHT **The various types of energy, or chi, present in and around a building.**

SNAKE ENERGY

Snake chi lies at the centre of a building. It is linked with the element earth and the central axis of the compass. Snake chi represents both stillness and movement.

TORTOISE ENERGY

Tortoise chi is the energy behind a building and may be a row of trees, a hill or a well-proportioned wall. The tortoise represents the past and what supports a structure and its occupants. The tortoise symbolizes the north, and the element water.

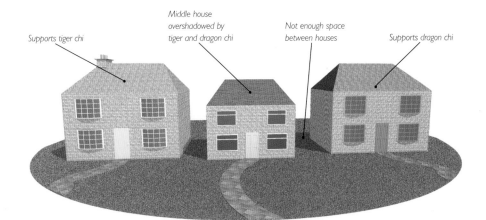

Supports tiger chi

Middle house overshadowed by tiger and dragon chi

Not enough space between houses

Supports dragon chi

LEFT **Tiger and dragon chi should support the sides of your home, but not overshadow it. These houses are too close together.**

TORTOISE ENERGY

What is behind the home is also very important. The area at the back of a building is traditionally known as 'The Tortoise' and will ideally offer strong, long-term support. A good support to tortoise chi could take the form of land rising up away from the building (from a point beyond the boundary line), or a carefully sited and well-proportioned brick wall. Another taller and more substantial building could do the same job, as long as there was no feeling of it overshadowing your space. Equally, a majestic, aged tree would achieve the same effect.

Good tortoise chi can be likened to sitting in a comfortable chair. Obviously you want clear space and something pleasant to look at in front of you, but what about to either side and behind? A decent chair will support your back, and afford some protection at the sides without making you feel closed in or cramped; a building needs the same kind of support.

BELOW **Tortoise chi is like the back of a chair – it gives comforting support without cramping the person using it. The occupants of a house need it to feel supported and able to approach life confidently.**

AN INSECURE PAST

A space with inadequate tortoise energy will suffer from an inability to hold chi. This will manifest itself in the building's occupants, who will experience feelings that lack support from those around them, and are unable to make any progress in life. If left unchecked, this

BELOW **A strong old tree behind a house can provide adequate tortoise chi. Inadequate tortoise energy behind a home may leave the occupants suffering from backache, fatigue and an inability to organize repairs or renovations.**

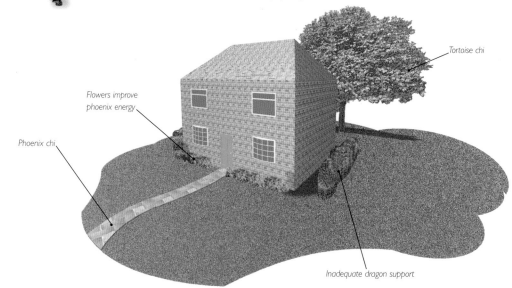

Flowers improve phoenix energy

Phoenix chi

Tortoise chi

Inadequate dragon support

ABOVE **This house has a bank of trees behind it and to the sides, providing its occupants with a sense of stability, strength and support. It may be no coincidence that such homes are often owned by people who are financially secure.**

could lead to symptoms as diverse as backache or fatigue, as well as an inability to organize repairs for the building, which will consequently slowly deteriorate.

People living in a space like this may come from backgrounds that did not nurture them in the ways that they needed. They may find it difficult to move on beyond feelings of being unsafe and anxious. The tortoise chi of a space tells us about the nature of our past. It can also alert us to the best Feng Shui to practise inside our home to compensate for any deficiencies outside.

When living in a home with deficient tortoise chi, for example where the land falls away at the back (perhaps as wide open or waste land, or a series of low, run-down buildings), it is even more important to arrange the layout of rooms and furniture to 'protect the back'. This means placing chairs with their backs away from door openings, walkways or open spaces in rooms, and avoiding performing any activity with your back to a doorway.

MAKING THE CHANGE

There are, of course, ways to transform the quality of tortoise chi. These remedies are not normally things that can be put into place overnight and you may have to be very creative. It is worth making a start with the placement of an object designed to signal to the universe that you have identified something in your life that you would like to change. For example, if you intend at some point to remedy your lack of tortoise chi by planting a row of trees or dense shrubbery behind your home, a symbolic plant of similar quality to the ones you eventually intend to use could be placed at the proposed planting site. Similarly a standing stone, or heavy object of some age and bearing, will start the work for you.

Creating tortoise energy is huge and wonderful work, building walls, erecting statues, and building up land. Meanwhile, a long look at your personal backup system, in other words friends, family and teachers who support you as you go through life, will invest the process with meaning and begin to make the transformation real.

To complete the Feng Shui picture, dragon and tiger energy at either side should not be restrictive: it should give protection and gently directive support.

ABOVE **If the land at the rear of your home slopes away, or has inadequate tortoise energy for any other reason, place a heavy statue, shrubbery, a wall or a row of trees there to help create tortoise chi.**

3

feng shui outside the home

TOP
10
QUESTIONS

Phoenix energy represents the south, but my front door faces west. Does this mean that my front door has south/fire energy, or west/metal energy?

I would read this as a west-facing door, which is ideal for relaxation, completion of projects, and rest.

The ground slopes gently downwards behind my house, and we have no garden to plant trees. How can we build some tortoise energy?

Concentrate on the inside of the house, if you have no back garden. Good quality window coverings, a beautiful, solid back door, and plenty of attention to detail in furniture placement will all help.

Our house is in a narrow, terraced street. We do not have a front garden. Is this a problem?

I would want to see a bright, well-kept, colourful building opposite. If traffic passes your door, hopefully it is slow-moving and not too busy. Keep your front door and its surroundings immaculate. Add a hanging basket and window boxes, and a subtle wind-chime just inside your front door.

The front door of my flat opens directly onto the staircase to the first floor – is this good or bad phoenix energy?

You need to do a little work here. Arrange the approach to your front door carefully, with a heavy doormat and two 'guardian' statues or plants. Bright, reflective door furniture will also help.

屋
外
之
風
水

I have flat, open spaces to either side of my house. Is this bad?

The lack of dragon/tiger support will mean you will have to be more independent, but try to avoid becoming too opinionated or dogmatic. Add structures or hedges to help create dragon/tiger energy. If the house faces east or west it will help.

I have no front door. My main door is at the side of the house. Is this where my phoenix chi is?

Yes. Many people have no front doors and use side or back doors instead. The door with the phoenix energy is the one that a first time visitor would approach, or the one that your friends consider to be your main door.

The front of our house looks out towards a hill. It is not close, but we can feel its 'presence'. Will this disturb our phoenix energy?

Yes. I worked on a house like this, and we solved the problem by changing the position of the front door. When the occupants started to use the back door as the main door, life improved.

I live in a flat in a tower block. There are other tall structures close by. How will this affect the phoenix, dragon, tiger and tortoise energy?

Look to what is on all sides of your flat in the same way as you would if you were living in a house. The other tall buildings close by could also be providing tortoise, dragon or tiger chi.

We live in a motor home. How does this affect our phoenix, dragon, tiger and tortoise energy?

It will all depend on where you park your home. Choose sites, if possible, that will give you good tortoise, dragon, tiger and phoenix energy. For example, you could park in front of a hill or building to give you some tortoise chi.

In the centre of our office building we have an atrium, an empty space lined with windows to let in the light. Does this mean we have no snake energy?

On the contrary, this is snake energy at its clearest. Make the most of this area, keeping it clean, bright and beautiful. Add a seat or two and sit there peacefully. It is an asset to your building.

4

clearing clutter

Before I sit down to write, I clear my desk. To some people the reason for doing this will be obvious. They may or may not be able to explain why they know it is important to do it, but it is something they do automatically like cleaning their teeth or changing their socks. These people would no more walk past a used plate and cup than they would ignore a crying child.

Other people feel they need to be surrounded with yesterday's paraphernalia in order to be able to function. They feel at home amongst an array of possessions. This morning's coffee cup, yesterday's mail and someone else's book are all essential ingredients of their work process. To them, to sit before an empty desk is to be deprived of a source of comfort and support, as barren an experience as an empty glass in a bar.

VOYAGE OF DISCOVERY

If we can agree that for each of us life offers a never-ending unfolding of opportunities to learn and to increase our awareness about ourselves and our unique connection to everything that exists, then we must already be aware that everyone is at a different stage of a very different journey from everyone else. However, Feng Shui can work for all of us, irrespective of our individual backgrounds, characters and paths in life.

If our practice of Feng Shui is to remain sound and valuable, then at its heart must remain close observation, heightened awareness of the nature of chi, and consistent practice. To create an environment that suits our individual needs, we can start by looking at the way we approach the minutiae of our lives, the things we choose to surround us and the way we organize those things.

CREATING A SUPPORTIVE ENVIRONMENT

If you are in your home or office, start by taking note of the objects that surround you – the things you can see and the things you cannot actually see but that you believe or know to be there. These may be items deliberately put out of sight in cupboards, drawers or other containers. Now move to another room. Add what you discover here to your earlier findings. You can stop after this, or you can continue the process all around your living space if you wish.

FAR LEFT **These bookcases make an attractive feature, but the large amount of books will cause chi to stagnate and create a feeling of heaviness in the room.**

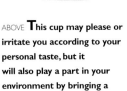

清除雜物

ABOVE **T**his cup may please or irritate you according to your personal taste, but it will also play a part in your environment by bringing a certain kind of energy with it.

ABOVE **I**t is important to become aware of the effect that particular objects have upon you. The angular, yet rounded shape of this cup mixes Yin and Yang energies.

ABOVE **T**he rounded shape of this cup, and its subdued tones, encourage calm, contemplation and stability. Its colours show a balance of the elements.

ABOVE **I**f you would like to introduce some more fire energy into your home or workplace, the angular edges and striking colours of this cup will help.

ABOVE **T**his cup combines the colours of water and earth. As earth controls water, this cup would help the user to feel more secure, or to make dreams a reality.

If you are wondering where all this is going and why it matters anyway, you need to think in terms of energy. We have got used to thinking about our space in terms of the quality and flow of chi. We are becoming used to the idea that we can change that chi, move it around, rebalance and in some way renegotiate it.

As our awareness becomes more heightened, we will begin to recognize the energetic implications of absolutely everything that surrounds us. This is something that most of us already practise to varying degrees. For example, most people know they will feel different wearing the blue shirt they have pulled out of the wardrobe to the red one they have left for another time; they will spend a few moments

choosing a new toothbrush, and they will opt to drink coffee from one cup rather than another. If we start to think of these choices in energetic terms, we understand why extending this practice and allowing it to become a series of consciously made choices will actually become a supportive process. This is not meant to suggest that we should adopt controlling and obsessive behaviour, but simply that we should have an awareness of why it might be more or less important at different times to do different things. In other words, we must give ourselves permission to create the environments that will really support and nurture us. (It helps us to understand why the crockery our friend gave us is such a source of irritation, and allows us to feel able to give it away!)

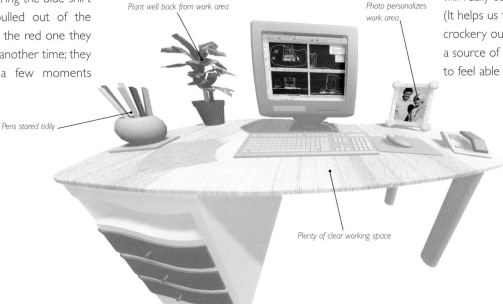

Plant well back from work area

Photo personalizes work area

Pens stored tidily

Plenty of clear working space

LEFT **A** tidy desk gives a sense of order, and can enable a person to think more clearly. On a practical level, it saves time because it enables people to find things quickly, but on an energy level it will also allow positive chi to flow more easily.

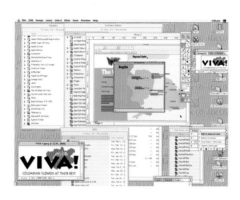

LEFT **It is also possible to have electronic clutter, so identify all the useful files stored in your computer and discard the rest.**

ABOVE **Clutter can accumulate in subtle places, so look to your address book and delete any entries you no longer use.**

ABOVE **Keeping an item that you no longer use, just because it is valuable, will be a source of negative energy, so get rid of those fur coats and family heirlooms.**

IDENTIFYING CLUTTER

It has become common to label as clutter those things that no longer have any practical or aesthetic purpose, but clutter is really about things being in the wrong place at the wrong time, or to put it another way, inappropriate Feng Shui.

The process of removing clutter from everyday life begins with being able to spot it. Identifying the first layer of clutter is fairly easy. Most people can walk into a space and see things that should not be there – items that have an obvious alternative location. For most people, this is simply a matter of tidying up and relocating a few things. Doing it may make us feel a little better in the short term – clearer, brighter and more energetic – but how can we take this one stage further so that the initial feeling goes deeper and lasts longer? The answer is to remove things from our energy field that are not supporting our energy. This means more than reorganizing things or putting them out of sight. It means removing them altogether and throwing them out, and this seemingly drastic measure is where, for many people, the difficulty begins.

UNFINISHED BUSINESS

If you are one of those people for whom clearing out, tidying, organizing and ruthless non-hoarding is effortless, then you may need to bear with the rest of us as we make slow and careful progress through this task. However, I have never met anyone who did not

ABOVE **The first thing most people notice in any environment is what blatantly does not belong there, such as rubbish on the ground, or intrusive advertising** **hoardings. Identifying more subtle clutter is more difficult. When in doubt, an item may be judged as superfluous if it does not support you in your activities.**

BELOW **D**o not keep tins of paint just in case you need to 'touch up' the decor in your home. They will eventually dry out and will not match the faded paintwork.

LEFT **G**ive your old books to a library or rehabilitation centre, or sell them to a secondhand bookshop.

清除雜物

ABOVE **R**ecycle old blankets and towels as bedding for your pet or rags for your workshop, and get rid of the rest.

ABOVE **B**uild breaks into your clutter-clearing schedule so that you can relax completely and forget about the mess around you for a while. Then you can return to the job feeling refreshed and energized.

have something to learn from this highly disciplined procedure. I can almost guarantee that somewhere in your life you have stored away a little bundle of things that reflects an area of unfinished business. The whole process of clutter clearing becomes a trail of revelations about the beliefs we hold and the paths we think we must tread.

We should begin by identifying clutter as those things that do not support or nurture our energy. Decide to start with the space in your home that you believe to be the most clutter-free. Make an agreement with yourself that you will work through one space at a time and not be side-tracked, and do not begin another space before you have completed the first one. Becoming side-tracked is a handy device for avoiding things we do not want to do, so take note when you suddenly think of popping something next door, or when you have a sudden desire to make coffee or give up on the whole thing. This will almost certainly signal that you have just spotted some major clutter. So build proper breaks into your schedule and allocate set amounts of time for the task.

Make this clean-up an important priority, and do not allow yourself to be interrupted by the telephone or the doorbell. There is, after all, no point in spending time and effort on Feng Shui, creating wonderful colour schemes and fine-tuning furniture placement, if your whole space is packed with clutter. In fact, eliminating clutter is so important that I often advise people to have a really thorough clear-out before starting to apply any Feng Shui.

MAKING A COMMITMENT

Choose a time when you know that you are feeling centred and strong. This way you will trust your decisions and you will be acting on the basis of positive, rather than negative, thought processes. Decisions made in anger or fuelled by resentment rarely do us much good. On days that we believe we can conquer the world, we probably can. If such days are rare for you, when they do come, clearing out a cupboard is probably the last thing you will want to do. If this is the case, try clearing your clutter in smaller amounts. Clearing out a single shelf or work surface one day may boost your energy enough for you to tackle a little more the next day.

Decide in advance how much you will be able to do, thinking in terms of areas of a room, rather than whole rooms, and be kind to yourself when you decide how much to take on. This way you will have a greater chance of achieving what you set out to do and the whole experience will be successful. You can always decide to do a bit more if you feel like it.

It is worth mentioning at this point that clutter clearing can make you feel so good that, once started, you may just want to go on and on. A frenzied throwing away of almost all that you possess is not, however, the object of the exercise. Maybe you will end up with a few, much loved possessions, but to get the most out of the whole process it is worth having some understanding of what we are clearing out and why. The creation of order and clarity, balance and joy is the real motivation behind clearing clutter.

It is also worth bearing in mind that any space you have cleared will need cleaning the same day, so the whole process requires considerable supplies of energy. Mark a date in your diary and make a commitment to start on that day. Also decide upon a timescale for clearing either a whole room in your space, or a section within a particular room. You could even decide to clear the entirety of your space by a specified date. Your ability, or inability, to stick to those schedules will tell you about your attitude to yourself, your level of commitment and, in broad terms, just how much of a problem or gift this whole process is for you. It can be very revealing to look again at the proposed completion date at a later stage and see just how much has, or has not, been achieved.

ABOVE **T**his work area has a certain order to it, but there are too many objects crowding the shelves, and the whole structure dominates the room.

To improve the energy and keep it flowing freely, clear out all the clutter and screen off the shelves from the room by fitting doors or adding blinds.

CLUTTER CHECKLIST

Make a commitment to clear clutter ☐
Choose a date to start clutter clearing ☐
Put the date in your diary ☐
Decide how much to tackle ☐
Agree a timescale ☐
Have refuse sacks and 3 boxes ready ☐
Work with the door closed ☐
Sit quietly for a few minutes first ☐
Work from top to bottom ☐
Does the item makes you feel good? ☐
Is the item useful? ☐

Unwanted gift

Withered plant

清除雜物

Table clutter

Pile of magazines

Unwanted heirloom

LEFT **Work round the room systematically, considering everything that you can see. Remember to include framed photographs, pictures hanging on the wall, books, magazines, ornaments and any withered plants or damaged items.**

HOW TO START

You will need copious amounts of very strong refuse sacks and three boxes or crates. A good sense of humour will make your task easier!

The way to clear clutter is very straight-forward and well tested. Start by going to your chosen site. If possible, close the door behind you. This will help heighten your awareness of what is really going on in the room. If something is in there that should not be, it will soon come to your attention if you are closeted in with it.

Sit quietly in the space for a few minutes, thinking about what you are going to do. Then move to sit by the doorway or entrance to the room. Avoid sitting with your back to the door; instead sit just to the left of the door facing into the room. This is where chi comes into the room and begins to travel around it. If you live in the southern hemisphere, you will need to sit to the right of the door. If you proceed from this position, the naturally occurring flow of chi will help you in your work.

Now begin to clear the clutter, starting with the very first thing you see as your eye travels clockwise (anticlockwise for the southern hemisphere) around the room. If you can, start with things high up and work downwards. Remember to include pictures, mirrors and objects attached to the ceiling, such as wind chimes or mobiles. Appraise your curtains and soft furnishings. Just how many of those CDs and tapes do you regularly listen to, and which are relics of another you, in another time and place? Is that sickly plant going to recover? Does your burgeoning video collection need weeding?

You need to ask yourself the same questions in relation to each item in the room:

- Does this item make me feel good?
- Do I enjoy owning it?
- Is it useful and creative for me?

It is worthwhile affixing the word 'now' to the end of these questions. Since we are aiming to facilitate change and growth, we need answers about how things are affecting us right now, not how we felt about them last year, last month, or even last week.

ABOVE **C**osmetics can accumulate into clutter at an alarming rate, so if you are harbouring a multitude of moisturizers or hair conditioners, think about the energy this may bring into your space. They will also be preventing positive chi from flowing freely, and the space they take up will not allow any exciting new qualities to enter your life.

COPING WITH THE PROCESS

As you begin to work on your space, you need to be aware that what you are dealing with is an energetic representation of yourself. The contents of each room will tell you a great deal about the person you are and the way you relate to your world.

A room absolutely crammed with objects is a reflection of one type of life; a room almost bare is a reflection of another. The contents of our bathroom, for example, will reveal our relationship to our body on a most intimate level. This is obvious, but what may be less obvious is exactly why we have fifteen lipsticks, or four different types of toothpaste, or why we keep so many bottles of hair conditioner.

As you work your way through the first room, the way you create energy around you will quickly become apparent. For example, do you hold onto a mass of items and therefore events, ideas and attitudes? Each object you keep in your space is a carrier for a whole series of energetic impulses. Everybody and every process that has had a part in its creation is still held there. The person who designed it, financed its creation, and took part in the making, marketing and retail distribution of it, the person from whom you purchased or received it, the shop where it was bought – they are all in there. Looking at the energetic package we are taking into our lives in this way brings the significance of clearing clutter into sharp perspective.

OBJECTS AND ENERGY

Try to visualize the difference between two chairs in a room. One is the product of a company run by a woman who dreamed of becoming a carpenter. For many years she trained under the careful watch of a master in the trade before setting up with a small group of people with pride in the integrity of their work. Wood is carefully selected from sustainable sources and brought to a workplace bright in chi energy, where it is carefully crafted and recreated as the chair you will eventually buy.

It is sold on to a retail outlet where the staff are happy and well motivated, a place you wander into, attracted by all the beautiful and interesting things you see inside. Within a few moments you see the chair – exactly what you have been looking for – and after an effortless exchange with a salesman you find that the chair can

FAR LEFT **C**ircumstances surrounding the purchase of an item will contribute to its energy. If it was crafted with pride and bought in a happy atmosphere, the energy will be better than if it was bought at a time of negativity.

easily be delivered to your home at a time that just happens to coincide with your day off from work. The whole experience, from start to finish, is a pleasure. Even the delivery man arrives just as you are preparing to do battle with an overgrown tree in your garden, and happens to be the brother of an excellent tree surgeon. A fantasy? Is life ever like this? Yes, for some people. It is all about the way we relate to the world we have created around us.

We could equally well have left our house one morning after a terrible argument with a friend, determined to buy the new chair, have driven in a state of anger and frustration to the first available furniture shop and imported a whole lot more trouble into our life. The poor product is of wood sourced from land that has been seriously abused for years, hacked into shape by a series of people who loathe their work and build resentment, irritability and pain into every joint and limb of the product. Add to this all the feelings and expectations we layer onto the object at that time. When we then take this chair home, we will have a seriously 'loaded' item.

CONSIDER THE SOURCE

In terms of energy, therefore, each item is a powerhouse of chi, but we can simplify the business of assessing each object and how to deal with it. If you feel negative about an item, for example, first consider its source, because the negativity may have something to do with where it came from. If you do not know the history of an item, you should trust your instinct.

ASSESSING GIFTS

Presents you receive from others can fall into several categories. The first, and probably easiest one to deal with, is the unwanted gift. This type of present may be something someone has given you after careful thought and perhaps much love. Whether you like it or dislike it, however, you may feel obliged to keep it because you do not want to hurt the giver's feelings.

The second type of present is the item somebody thought you might like, because he or she no longer has room for it. In my experience it is very often a piece of soft furnishing that we then sit on daily, absorbing all the chi it holds – drip-feeding the giver's

energy into our life. Clothing often passes between people in a similar way. Happily complicit, the unthinking recipient then wonders why he or she has so much difficulty finding the right partner, job or life.

The third type of present is the 'lifetime obligation' gift, inherited from a family member, and loaded with the duty to continue a whole set of family traditions. It could be anything from a bedstead or blanket box, to a set of screwdrivers. It often sits in our space as something we are going to 'pass on' to our children. Piles of yellowed and ageing books are often kept to be handed down to a bewildered generation who have more recent information at their fingertips.

All of these 'gifts' carry energy from the people giving them to you, and some will be weighted with responsibilities or expectations that you may not wish to have, or to fulfil. You should therefore consider each present carefully before allowing it to remain in your home or your workspace.

Disposing of clutter can be a wonderful chance to face up to unfinished business, clearing the way for new opportunities. Chuck out your old college books and you will find new learning coming into your life. Remove your redundant business suits and you may find that the job you really want to do involves wearing a wetsuit.

ABOVE **If you have always disliked a vase that was given to you as a present, steel yourself to be ruthless and get rid of it.**

ABOVE **Consider carefully before accepting cast-off clothes; when you wear them you will absorb the owner's energy.**

ABOVE **Think again before you agree to look after someone's possessions, even if they are only garden tools to be stored in your shed.**

BELOW **Give suitable unwanted items to a charity shop: someone else can benefit from your clear-out too.**

ABOVE **If you do not like the waste involved in throwing items away, take them to a recycling centre. Don't plan a car boot sale, because you will be tempted to keep items until you can sell them.**

MAKING DECISIONS

It is now time to label the three boxes we set out at the beginning. In the first box we will put the things we are definitely going to move on (get rid of); the second will be our seven-day decision box, and the third is the emotionally charged, too-hot-to-handle box – this is for items we know are symptomatic of some emotional tie.

THE MOVING-ON BOX

We will need to detach ourselves from any thought of benefiting from the things in this box. It is usually inappropriate to sell them: I have known people who, having successfully cleared a whole house of clutter, delayed the completion of the process in the hope of being able to sell some, if not all, of the cleared items. The effort of selling then takes over from the energetic job of keeping the items, while the objects in question remain in a storage area indefinitely.

It is even less likely that anyone you know will benefit from your unwanted items. Offer them to no one unless you make it absolutely clear what they are taking on.

Charity shops will take almost any item and attempt to sell it for a good cause. Recycling in this way can be a good route for any items that you feel are too good to throw away.

Once we have decided to remove the clutter from our lives, we have already made huge steps towards disentangling our energy from it and all that it signifies. However, it is not enough simply to identify the clutter and move it out of sight into the back of a cupboard or up into the attic. We must recognize how it is holding us back and that we must remove it completely from our energetic sphere.

It should be easy to get rid of things once we have finished with them. Difficulty in removing an object from our space tells us that we have not fully recognized what it is we are dealing with or what we can learn from the item, or why we bought it. It usually helps if we acknowledge our responsibility for attracting an item in the first place. A mental word of thanks for the lesson we have learnt and an acknowledgement that we are ready to let it go is often all that is needed to get the object through that hard-to-pass front door.

BELOW **When dealing with an unwanted gift from a well-intentioned giver, make a note of the item in a notebook and give it a 'sell-by' date, after which time you can discard it without guilt.**

When dealing with unwanted gifts, it helps to recognize the intention of the giver. For example, the person may have wanted to give you something humorous, pretty or useful. Decide how long you need to keep the item in order to appreciate the giver's kindness. Once you have passed this self-imposed 'sell-by' date, you can remove the item without guilt. It is important to look after your own needs and acknowledge that, if the original givers of the item care for you unconditionally, they will be the first to applaud your decision to remove it from your energetic sphere. It often happens that, if one person sets an example of moving unwanted items on, other people feel freer to follow suit.

THE SEVEN-DAY DECISION BOX

Everyone works through the clearing process at a different speed. There are no prizes for speedy completion, partly because a true clutter-free moment can never arrive. It is an ongoing process. However, if there are items you simply cannot decide whether or not to keep, set yourself a deadline for making a decision. The deadline may be half an hour or a week, but the important thing is that you have set the decision process in motion. During this time, just be absolutely honest about the things you are considering and then be kind to yourself about how you deal with them. This does not mean that you end up keeping a lot more clutter and emotional debris, simply that you are creating for yourself a situation that will enable you to let go of things appropriately.

RIGHT **If you no longer have a use for an item but it has sentimental value, you may need more time to decide about letting it go. In a sense, you are clearing your emotional debris.**

LEFT **If you have kept an old teddy bear, and the childhood memories it rekindles make you unhappy, put it in the 'too-hot-to-handle box' so that you can take longer to consider the emotional reasons behind your decision to keep it.**

THE TOO-HOT-TO-HANDLE BOX

At any point in the clearing process, you may notice that your need to divert yourself from the job in hand has become more extreme. You may become tempted to go out and walk the dog, visit the gym, do some shopping or telephone a friend. This is the moment to look very carefully at the items of clutter that are nearby. Our emotional resistance to dealing with certain items can be huge. For example, the prospect of getting rid of the bed we slept in with an ex-partner, the record collection that was our only friend during lonely teenage years, or the tennis rackets we bought as part of an unfulfilled ambition to become a great player, can be hard.

Acknowledging that life needs to move on is not easy. Mothers who encourage grown-up children to keep childhood toys, partners who persuade you to keep the wedding dress their mother was married in, single people with a house full of items designed for one, when they are now ready to share their lives, are all people who could use the too-hot-to-handle box.

Recognizing the reasons for keeping things that do not make us feel entirely comfortable is a very good start. Setting such objects aside and then beginning to deal with the emotions that surround them is powerful work. The items that go into this box are those we cannot bear to discard, even though we know that hanging on to them is no longer right for us. Once we have looked at the emotional reasons for keeping these things, we can move to a point where we can let go of them altogether.

清除雜物

MAINTAINING A CLUTTER-FREE LIFE

Now that you have assessed your life in terms of the energy you choose to have around you, a large part of your time will be spent keeping it as uncluttered as possible. The ongoing clearing of clutter will become a habit, like taking a shower, or cleaning your teeth. Also, having experienced life in an increasingly clutter-free zone, you will be keen to keep the clarity level rising.

ANTI-CLUTTER LORE

■ Never acquire new things as the result of a compromise, or through a feeling of being rushed or pressured.

■ Always check your motive before making a new acquisition.

■ If you know you buy things on impulse, never make a purchase without leaving the shop for a given amount of time first. If necessary, allow yourself a controlled number of purchases that will live in a 'reassessment zone' of your home. That way you can identify what is going on.

■ If someone is giving something away, look carefully at your motive for taking it on.

■ When you are receiving a present, attend carefully to the moment it changes hands. By observing this exchange, you will learn a lot about what you may end up doing with it.

■ Be aware that today's joyful purchase may end up as tomorrow's problem item. This will slow down your purchase of clutter considerably. You will also be playing your part in reducing consumer demand and the rapid turning of our resources into mountains of waste.

■ Always consider very carefully before you agree to store or look after anything for anyone else.

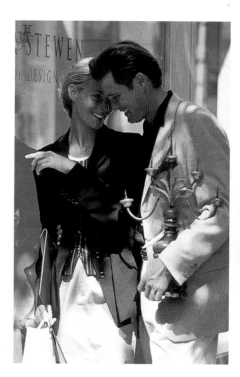

RIGHT **C**learing clutter from the home and the workplace releases people from the emotional pull of the past and enables them to make room for new relationships and fresh projects. It can also boost energy levels.

REDUCE CLUTTER AND CHANGE YOUR LIFE

The first thing that most people notice when they begin to pay more attention to the energetic make-up of their environment is that their energy level rises. As different areas of our space become clearer, so do parts of our body, mind and spirit. You will soon learn whereabouts in your house to look in order to clear and brighten up various aspects of your mental and physical being, and therefore your life. Many people find that clearing their kitchen and bathroom will give their physical being a boost, while a simple matter of energy depletion can be remedied by looking to the bedroom. An attic full of junk will interfere with spiritual growth and disempower people

LEFT **P**hotographs also have a 'shelf life'. Flip through your albums, and discard any photographs that now seem to belong to a time that is no longer relevant to your life. Photographs can accumulate into clutter very quickly, and should be cleared out regularly.

清除雜物

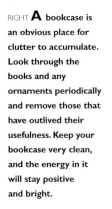

RIGHT **A** bookcase is an obvious place for clutter to accumulate. Look through the books and any ornaments periodically and remove those that have outlived their usefulness. Keep your bookcase very clean, and the energy in it will stay positive and bright.

LEFT **A**ccording to Feng Shui, an attic full of junk is believed to interfere with spiritual growth and to cause people to suffer a loss of power personally and professionally. The heavily-loaded energy in the roof can also obstruct the aspirations of the occupants below.

on all sorts of levels. A lack of opportunities should take you to examine your front door and entrance hall, because these areas represent the chances that enter your life. If there are problems with children, look carefully at the areas where they spend a lot of time. This is more than just clearing out and throwing away things you have outgrown in some way; it involves changing the fundamental way that you live in your space. It will make you think carefully about what you bring into your space and the way it changes the dynamic of your life.

The pursuit of simplicity, clarity and wholeness becomes effortless in an environment that reflects clutter-free principles. A space filled with a complicated array of discordant, muddy energetics is not a place conducive to wellbeing. It must be said, however, that there are times when we all need to slow down, or even shut off completely from striving for a streamlined, clutter-free existence, where Feng Shui is carefully applied to maximum effect. Working with chi energy is not about on/off switches, lists of rules, or categorization into good and bad. Very often a part of someone's

growth process will involve a spiralling away from clarity and potentially painful, bright chi. This is not a time to become judgemental about that person's need to clear clutter.

In fact, a good reminder to us all not to become clutter-busting proselytes, is to imagine someone else's possible perspective on our own clutter, whether it is easy to see or hidden away, and to keep looking to our own environment for potential pockets of cluttered energy. For example, when did you last remove redundant contacts from your address book, or clear out your old computer files or disks? Inspect your photograph albums, keep a watchful eye on bookcases that get piled high with all manner of junk. Investigate the bottom of the garden, which mysteriously attracts rusting wheelbarrows and paint cans, and delightful offerings from the neighbourhood cats. Check less obvious sources of clutter, such as the jewellery on your hand or round your neck. It may tell you more about your lack of success in forming healthy new relationships than a full-blown clutter-bust right the way through your home.

4

clearing clutter

TOP **10** QUESTIONS

清除雜物

I have a box with old letters and postcards. I still read them from time to time, and they give me a lot of pleasure. Am I doing myself harm by keeping them?

Absolutely not. Honouring and treasuring the past can give you great support – it is tortoise energy in action. Always follow your feelings, but if these items ever start to feel outdated or you stop using them, discard them.

I have a number of valuable antiques left to me by a relative. I feel obliged to keep them but something about them makes me feel depressed. Should I get rid of them?

Yes, especially as they are depressing you. If the potential financial loss of removing them is worrying you, then this is one of the few occasions when I would recommend selling them.

What should I do with things that I know I will need in the future, but that are cluttering up my space?

If you really will need these things in the future but need to store them now, for example skis during the summer months, then it is simply a question of organizing appropriate storage, and by this I mean accessible, roomy and ordered space used specifically for storage.

I cannot bring myself to get rid of my childhood teddy. Do I have to part with it?

No, you do not need to if it brings back happy memories. Allow yourself to mature into adulthood in an appropriate way and your relationship with your teddy bear will change from a devoted friend and security item to a much-loved souvenir.

清除雜物

A friend has asked me to look after her sofa until she finds a larger home. What should I do?

Do you want to store it? Probably not, but there is often guilt to be overcome. Would you ask a similar favour of her, especially in the light of what you know about energetics? Or would you pay to put it into storage? Tell your friend that you value the friendship far too much to oblige, and ask her to consider why she is hanging onto her sofa!

I have a lot of photographs and books that take up a lot of space, but I cannot seem to get rid of them. What would you suggest?

Look carefully at your reasons for wanting to keep them. What do they represent for you? If you are really stuck, ask an enlightened friend to help you go through them and realize that getting rid of them completely may take some time.

I have heard that clearing clutter can help people to lose weight. Is this true and, if so, how does it work?

For some people, carrying body weight is like holding onto energy. This is a way of remaining at a stage in life where, for some reason, they got stuck. For these people, clearing clutter helps them move on and they will no longer need the extra weight.

I would challenge anyone to find clutter in my flat. It is minimalist, but some people have said it is extreme. Is it possible to have too little clutter?

No, you can never have too little clutter. Check your motives for having your space so sparse. Could it reflect something in your life that doesn't bear scrutiny, or do you just love clarity? Trust yourself to do what is right for you.

What happens if I later find I have thrown away something vital?

This does not happen, but you may believe it has. If you were to be given back that item, you would see why it is not right for the job you now have for it. It might not fit comfortably or do its job properly. It would also block an opportunity for you to do things differently. This happened to me, then I was offered a replacement by someone who has since become a friend.

Isn't it wasteful to get rid of so many things when so many people have so little?

Only if as soon as you get rid of them, you bring in the next load. Once we stop needing to use possessions to fulfil a lack in ourselves, we will no longer be held in a vicious circle of accumulation. Clearing clutter is no more wasteful than refusing to smoke a cigarette that someone has mistakenly lit for you.

5

tuning
your
space

As your sensitivity to energy increases and you become increasingly aware of the chi of your space, there will inevitably be a moment when you walk into a room and feel that something major has happened there. A cursory glance around may tell you that nothing in the room has physically changed from the last time you were there, and yet something feels remarkably different. The air may be sweeter and more resonant. The outlines of various objects may have become clearer, as though a muddy haze has cleared and brought everything into sharper focus. There will almost certainly be an acute sense of emptiness in the room, which may lead you to look for something that is missing, and yet the room will feel at the same time wonderfully complete and restful.

Familiarizing yourself with this new territory can be a little unnerving. It is very likely that, if you think back, you will notice that the change in the room has followed an atmospheric shift in the climate, or a fairly major event in or around that space. A thunderstorm, the passing of the spring equinox, or the dropping of a strong south-westerly wind could all produce this effect; so could a shift of energy brought about by the revelation of a hidden truth, or the coming together of people who have been physically separated for a long time, or the departure of somebody who has had a big impact on the remaining residents. For whatever reason, the energy of the space has changed and now resonates with greater clarity.

ENERGY IN TUNE

A really clear and finely tuned space is so healing that people will feel different as soon as they enter it. Everyone will be able to report something beneficial, whether it is a sudden return of appetite, a rush of happiness and feeling of goodwill, the immediate solution to a problem, or a more low-key feeling of relaxation. The clarity and energy of the room will also allow the occupants to shed any emotional and energetic debris and to feel better afterwards.

Good Feng Shui in a building will help a space to keep itself naturally cleared and tuned. In fact, in certain buildings and spaces, the level of clarity and resonance can become so overwhelming that people can experience spontaneous healing, or insights that become visionary in their intensity. This quality is at the heart of much sacred

FAR LEFT **A lightning storm may produce about the shift in energy that good Feng Shui is said to bring to a building or inhabited space. Greater clarity and resonance may be felt immediately by those who enter it.**

architecture: the design of these wondrous buildings, coupled with the use of sound and colour, resonates with sparkling energy.

Awareness of the nature of chi helps the Feng Shui practitioner to create structures that will tune the energy flowing within them. We do not need all buildings to be created for the same purpose; however, architects should bestow all structures and their rooms with the ability to be energetically clear for day-to-day living and working. A wonderful sense of purpose and energy within each room should be available to everyone through the building's location, design and time of construction – in short, the Feng Shui of the space.

Most people are able to appreciate the cleansing nature of the moment before dawn or the turning of the tide, but the impact of a new moon or a change in the wind's direction has been forgotten by most of us. We have also lost our understanding of many traditional space-clearing practices, and we may explain away such techniques as either outdated superstition or purely practical actions. For example, the customs of sweeping the front of a house with a new broom, carrying coal over the threshold on New Year's Day, or throwing a pinch of spilt salt over the left shoulder are still remembered, and sometimes still practised, but our knowledge of the reasoning or motives behind these actions has almost disappeared. All are basically concerned with keeping the energy levels of a space at their most positive and beneficial. In the same way, we have forgotten how to maintain clean, bright energy in our homes and workspaces. Keeping the spaces we inhabit clear and energized enables us to bring into our lives the same dynamic energy that can be found in many of the sacred buildings of the world.

ABOVE **A**n architect who is aware of good **Feng Shui principles will take into account the time the building is to be constructed, its purpose and** location, and consider design, colour, decoration and materials, as well as the auditory and visual effect upon those who will use it.

RIGHT **E**nergetic debris collects at floor level, particularly in corners, so washing floors gives a quick energetic boost to a space.

57

ABOVE **If arguments break out continually in a home, they imply that something in the building is obscuring clear communication between its inhabitants. The remedy is to clear and tune the chi of the whole living space.**

HARMONY AND DISCORD

Once they have experienced the difference between a space with tuned energy and one in disharmony, most people would wish to avoid spending time in the latter. Very often people will avoid a place with a bad atmosphere, acknowledging that something unpleasant has happened there, and will keep away until things improve. It is often not possible, however, to leave a space to clear itself. Intervention is needed, but how do we know when a space needs an energetic transformation? The most obvious signal will be that it simply does not feel right, in spite of every effort to make it feel welcoming. Having cleared the clutter, cleaned everywhere, plumped the cushions and added flowers, it may still feel flat and uninspiring.

CANDIDATES FOR SPACE CLEARING

Any room in the home or workspace can need space clearing and tuning, even after all the clutter has been removed and the area has been cleaned. For example, a kitchen may make the occupant feel very slightly nauseous or confused, a bathroom may never seem to do its job of making a person feel clean and fresh, and a bedroom may simply create a cacophony of disordered thought and unease. Playrooms where children lie slumped on the floor, offices where communications are lost and muddled, dining rooms where people never enjoy a hearty meal, or houses that visitors can never find or that never make them feel welcome, are all obvious candidates for space clearing. Gardens also need space clearing.

HOW TO SPOT A DISCORDANT SPACE

- Sudden and sometimes unexplained breakages.
- The need for unrealistic amounts of cleaning.
- Occupants not being able to communicate clearly and easily.
- Disturbed sleep or appetite.
- A guest suddenly leaving after a shorter than expected stay.
- A whole series of light bulbs blowing, or unexplained water leaks or breakdowns of electrical appliances and heating systems.
- Computers crashing, and technical equipment 'playing up'.

調節空間

OTHER OCCASIONS FOR SPACE CLEARING

■ When moving into a new space, and before leaving an old one.
■ When a baby is born.
■ When a person or a pet dies.
■ When someone is unwell.
■ When two people part.
■ All rites of passage, including puberty, coming of age, marriage, menopause, retirement.
■ After a major accident or upheaval.
■ When setting up a new business venture.

ABOVE **F**amily pets are also affected by the chi of a home, and how they behave towards you and interact with each other can give you a lot of valuable information about the quality of energy in your home.

I would also recommend clearing and tuning your space at the New Year, summer and winter solstice, spring and autumn equinox, before a birthday celebration, and after cutting down a large tree or powerful plant in the immediate vicinity, even when it is cut down by someone else and is not even on your land.

There will be other occasions when space clearing and tuning is needed, and in these cases it is usually best to follow your intuition as much as possible.

ABOVE **W**hen a baby is born into a home, it is essential to clear and tune the house because a shift in energy occurs when someone or something new appears. Creating a peaceful environment in which energy can flow smoothly will also encourage the growth of a healthy, happy baby.

TRUST YOUR INSTINCT

When working with energy, awareness needs to be heightened and feelings listened to intently – just like a fox will lock on to a scent, with the accuracy of the radar on a destroyer. Children, whose minds are uncluttered by the need to explain and justify, are particularly good at spotting wrinkles in energetic patterning. They are also the first to display symptoms of energetic imbalance, so a whining child, or one who is always clumsily knocking into things, could be telling you that the space needs clearing and tuning. Pets can also warn you of a potential energy problem: dogs become warm around their heads, and cats forget where they should go to the toilet.

PREPARING TO CLEAR A SPACE

Clearing a space means transforming its energetic patterns to bring it into a state of balance and clarity. It is like cleaning a house, but in terms of energy rather than physical cleanliness. Tuning a space means setting the energy to work for a specific purpose. It is like rearranging the furniture, in energetic terms. Major space clearing and tuning is a job for someone who is very comfortable with tracking energy, but anyone can learn to do a simple clearing session to improve the energy of a room. Once adept at this level, you can make a careful progression towards more profound work, but if you are in doubt, call in someone with more experience to help you.

When you are ready to begin, sit quietly and comfortably in the space you are going to clear, until you feel at ease and your breath is flowing naturally. Breathe in through your nose and out through your mouth. Relax your jaw, stomach muscles and face.

Now you need to decide where, energetically, the room begins. This has nothing to do with the position of doorways or windows. Trust your first instinct and be guided by your feelings, even if it means you end up working in the fireplace or squeezed behind the sofa. You are looking for a place from which to unwind the room's energy, and where you can keep your space-clearing equipment – it will be your workstation and the energetic boundary of the room.

You will need a space-clearing kit to help you clear the room's energy and alter its vibrational level. You can use anything you feel may be helpful for this task, or you can try the items suggested below. Your kit should be carefully chosen and cared for with respect. Store it in silk cloth in an elevated place. Never keep something once you have an indication that it has done its work for you. Such an indication might be dropping it, a blemish or crack appearing, any change in smell, appearance or texture, or repeated difficulty in finding it. Also, do not be tempted to use your space-clearing tools for any other purpose.

TIPS ON PREPARATION

■ Decide on the limits of the space you want to clear.
■ Choose a time for doing this work. Give yourself a time limit – you will clear the space for that amount of time and no longer.
■ Clarify in your mind your motive for clearing.
■ Prepare yourself by drinking some good quality water, remove your watch and change into some really comfortable clothes that can be cleaned easily when you have finished your work.

SPACE-CLEARING KIT

1. Incense or smudge stick (available from New Age or Native American stores).
2. A small bowl of fresh water.
3. A bell with a clear, resonant tone.
4. A candle (let your instincts choose the colour).
5. Five pebbles or small stones.
6. A handful of sand.
7. A handful of earth, salt or rice, and a cotton or silk cloth (not pictured below).

BELOW **Clearing a space means balancing energies within it, while tuning means rearranging the energies for a functional purpose. A space-clearing kit will help you to purify the energies. Tools like the ones pictured here can be useful for this work.**

BASIC SPACE-CLEARING PROCEDURE

Once you have chosen the place for your workstation, spread the cloth over it and set out the items from your space-clearing kit. Use your instincts to choose which items to use first, or follow the sequence below. This method also works outside.

1 First, work with the sand to ground the space. Take a small handful of sand and scatter a fine line all around the boundary of the space you are clearing. Alternatively, let a few grains drop from your hand in five places as you walk around the edge of the room, starting at your workstation, skirting the entire perimeter of the space, and completing your trip back to the workstation. As you walk, be acutely aware of the way you are moving. If you find that you are holding your breath, pay special attention to that part of the space. Try to get used to sensing the quality of chi you are moving through, tracking the energetic flow for changes in quality or direction. Simply noticing the change in energy is all that is needed to effect a transformation.

ABOVE **L**ighting a candle will add illumination and energy to your work.

2 Now pick up the pebbles or stones and retrace your steps, placing a pebble or stone at each of five places on your route. They can be deposited in the same five places as the grains of sand, or you can choose different spots for them.

ABOVE **P**ut pebbles on your path as you walk around your home.

3 Back at the workstation, light the candle with the clear intention of it helping the space clearing – this is rather like making a wish. Leave the candle burning while you continue your task – it will give illumination as well as adding fire energy to your work.

4 Next take the bell and walk in a meandering route around the room, slowly ringing the bell so that its sound permeates the entire space, high and low, into corners and recesses, until you can feel the energy becoming clearer.

5 Return to your workstation, sit quietly and wait for a few minutes, and try to sense what is happening in the room.

6 When you feel calm and energized, scatter the water into the corners and boundaries of the room, leaving the bowl in a position well away from your workstation. The water will clear the deep, hidden energy of the room. Blocked or stagnant emotion will begin to flow and allow the room's energy to lift and transform. All remaining pieces of equipment should be in your hand or at the workstation.

7 Now complete the transformation of the room with scented smoke. You can light the incense alongside the candle, or light a smudge stick (a bunch of aromatic herbs) and waft it around the room before returning it to burn at the workstation. Do not leave burning candles or smudge sticks unattended at any time.

8 Use the earth, salt or rice to complete the work: scatter it around the boundary line or simply pile it at any doorway.

9 Return to the workstation and sit quietly before putting away your tools in the reverse order to the way you used them, but leave all the scattered grains and the salt in position for about 24 hours before clearing away. Blow out the candle and fold away the cloth. Thank the space as you leave, and let it settle while you go and wash your hands and face and maybe change your clothes.

BELOW **S**it quietly for a few minutes before putting away your tools.

SPACE CLEARING AT A DEEPER LEVEL

The space-clearing technique I have just described is the easiest way for someone to begin working with energy, and will lay a good foundation for continued learning, whether or not a person has an instinct for such work. To track energy effectively, you need faith in yourself and your ability to do the job. Like attracts like, and any element you bring to your work will be attracted into the space you are clearing in greater quantities.

THE NEXT STEP

If you feel happy working with energy in this way, you may decide to tackle a slightly more profound job in order to effect a deeper level of transformation. This could be something that you do to clear a space after an argument, or when someone is a little unwell. It may be just enough to clear someone's mind sufficiently to make a good decision on an important issue, or to balance the energy in a room to help someone sleep. If it has the happy effect of working at a deeper level still, this is fine, but it is best to safeguard a new practitioner, and the space, by limiting the intention to something fairly superficial.

During this process you will be simultaneously clearing and tuning the space. The structure can be kept similar to that of the first space-clearing procedure but, in order to increase the power of what you are doing, you must take more care in the preparation.

CONNECTING WITH A SPACE

Choose a time at least 24 hours before you intend to start the work, and establish your intention to bring about the transformation. To do this, take some time to consider what particular quality you would like the space to contribute to your life. For example, it could be a place for calm and reflection, or a space to meet with friends. You could ask for the space to provide you with exactly what you need, and leave the definition of that open.

Aim to make your ideas into a succinct intention, then try to reduce this to five words, or fewer if possible. On a clean piece of paper, write down exactly what you have decided, sign and date it, and then place it in the space.

RIGHT **C**lapping will disperse the negative energy in a room, especially the stagnant chi that accumulates in corners. Any kind of sound sends ripples of vibration through the atmosphere and will affect the energy there.

ABOVE **Y**ou can help someone to recover from an illness by rearranging and balancing things in the room in which he or she spends the most time. To discover what is needed, determine which kind of activity you would like the space to support, and then set a time to 'tune into' it.

From this moment until the completion of the job, watch carefully how you feel, and notice everything that happens to you. Between now and the beginning of the job you are gathering information that will be invaluable once you begin the practicalities. You and the space are now linked. If you experience an unusual, raging thirst, for instance, you will need water during your task the next day; if you feel oddly absent and light-headed, take more sand and stone to ground the energy. Your experience of working with the five transforming energies (see page 21) will really support your instincts.

By the time you are ready to begin working directly with the energy, you will have a good idea of what is needed. Having opened a dialogue with the space, you have already begun the work.

INCREASING AWARENESS

At the appointed time, set up your workstation in the usual way and begin to work with the space. Allow any change of feeling, emotional or physical, to register briefly and then pass through you. Visualize yourself releasing energy as you breathe out through your mouth. As you work, be aware of temperature changes or tingling sensations in your body. When you notice them, work more carefully and with more love. You may experience a need to spend more time in a certain area, to miss out a stage, or even to return to a spot. You may also feel that the room needs another quality entirely. Here are some suggestions to bring additional qualities into the space:

Sound: clap, sing, chant, or use musical instruments such as a drum, flute or different type of bell.

Breathing: gently blow into corners or simply stand still in a part of the room, breathing in easily through the nose and out through the mouth.

Objects: place plants, rocks or a bowl of water in parts of the room that feel appropriate.

Fresh air: open windows or doors as necessary, to allow an easier flow of energy.

Fire energy: light a fire or add more candles.

As before, return all your tools and leave the space to settle down. This time you will need to take a shower, change your clothes and rest a little before continuing with your day.

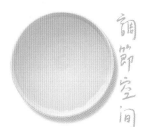

ABOVE **P**repare to use more water in your task if you feel unusually thirsty beforehand.

ABOVE **P**lants bring additional living energy into a space and help to keep the chi flowing smoothly and freely.

ABOVE **Y**ou may feel the need to place stones or rocks in certain areas. Follow your instincts.

ABOVE **S**weeping and washing floors will provide a good basis for clearing any negative chi that accumulates at ground level. Basic housekeeping practice often supports good Feng Shui and space-clearing procedures.

CLEANING WITH LOVE

Working with our space is something we can do every day. Once space clearing has become second nature to us, tuning should evolve naturally. Basic space-clearing techniques could be described as good housekeeping practice – clearing away our energetic debris. Our approach to cleaning our space is very important, and a routine is essential. Energetic debris collects low down in a space and hangs around in corners and recesses, therefore regular sweeping and washing of floors is invaluable.

Avoid harsh chemical cleaners and look into the cleaning and disinfecting properties of essential oils instead. For example, citrus and lavender oils are good disinfectants, and eucalyptus oil is good for bathrooms and sinks. Using natural products for cleaning can involve more effort, but consider the different dynamic between someone scrubbing a kitchen table with lemon juice, and someone standing back and spraying it with a chemical cleaner. Pour bleach down the toilet if you must, but why not polish your furniture with beeswax, even if it takes a little more effort? Putting love and energy into a home is about more than lighting a candle once a week.

Make the effort to walk into each room and put some loving energy into it every day. Choose furnishings and floor and window coverings with care. Natural tiles or wood, and rugs made from wool or cotton that can be shaken outside, are wonderful for keeping energy clear. Simple, strong window covers that can be changed with the seasons, bedding that can be taken out to air, windows that are opened regularly, all help to keep a space clear.

You could also decide to keep electrical pollution to a minimum by reducing your use of electrical equipment. And why not consider using an open fire or wood burner for heating some areas? Assigning a separate area for hanging outdoor clothes, and encouraging your guests to use it too, ensures your indoor space will quickly become your sanctuary. Your home is your castle, and you can make it as beautiful, uplifting, and resonant with energy as you wish. The way you connect to your space, at this basic level, can be very powerful.

BELOW **U**se beeswax and other natural methods to polish your home and improve its energies. Essential oils and natural cleansers, such as fresh lemon juice and vinegar, can also alter your home's energies in the same way as lighting a candle or opening a window can change the chi.

調
節
空
間

The things you do in your home and the way you do them are also important. If you only use your space to sit in, watch TV and eat take-away food, it will not be a vibrant place. A space needs to be home to a whole range of activities, sounds and events. Living a balanced and fulfilled life will set up energy patterns that will keep your living space clear of negative energies. This is why a really good party will often clear a tight, overcontrolled space more effectively than anything else, or why a good argument is said to clear the air.

IMPROVED INTUITION

After a period of following these rules of good practice, you will find it becomes easier to spot when the energy of a place is not clear. The notion of being able to sense what is needed to clear a space will become less obscure. It is a bit like changing the quality of the food you eat. If you start to exclude foods grown with the use of chemicals, and processed foods, and change to organically grown wholefoods, your receptivity to taste will improve. You will soon notice the difference if served the former, and will even be able to identify the offending ingredients.

THE FULLY-FLEDGED SPACE TUNER

Tuning a space relies on the ability to track energy very precisely. It is wonderful and powerful work. However, the ability to witness and release streams of energetic connections that will free a space (in a building or on land) for a new purpose, comes with experience and practice. The confidence and presence of mind required to tune a space is built from continuous adherence to good practice and recognition of a space's energetic dimension.

ABOVE **E**nsuring that clothing and rooms are well aired is an important part of purifying and redirecting energies in a building.

The things you do and the manner in which you do them have an effect on the kind of atmosphere you create within your home.

BELOW **A** home may suffer from electrical pollution. Restrained use of electrical appliances may keep this to a minimum, and you may consider replacing many of them with manual alternatives.

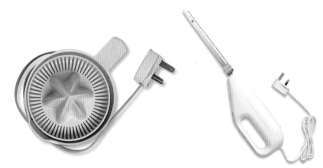

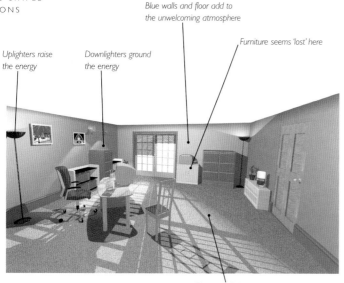

Uplighters raise
the energy

Downlighters ground
the energy

Blue walls and floor add to
the unwelcoming atmosphere

Furniture seems 'lost' here

The room feels too
large and uninviting

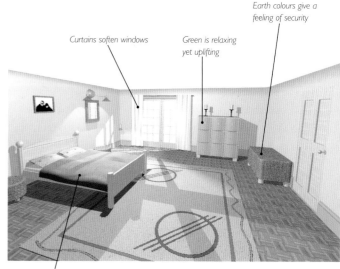

Curtains soften windows

Green is relaxing
yet uplifting

Earth colours give a
feeling of security

Bed has good view of windows
and door

DEDICATING A SPACE TO A FUNCTION

As a space becomes clearer, its true nature or purpose begins to emerge. This can happen in a number of ways. It may suddenly become very obvious to you that a room you had been struggling to decorate and arrange as a bedroom should have been used for an entirely different purpose all along. Or you may find that you can reposition the furniture in a way you would never previously have imagined feasible, and transform a difficult room into one that works perfectly. Likewise, it may suddenly become clear that family members should swap bedrooms in order for the layout of the house to work more effectively and harmoniously.

ABOVE LEFT **The home office in the top left picture clearly works better as a bedroom, as the top right illustration shows. In the top left picture, the office furniture seems** somewhat lost within the large space of the room, whereas the bedroom furniture pictured adjacent fits in well with the room and complements its airy spaciousness.

ABOVE RIGHT **After clutter and confused energies are cleared, you may find that the room's true nature and purpose is different from what you had imagined it to be.**

These are all Feng Shui problems and the solutions have been revealed by working purely at an energetic level. The realizations about the space may come as an absolute revelation: a solution to problems you had been struggling with for years. Perhaps at some point you even considered arranging the space in this way, but disregarded it as impossible.

NATURAL ORDER

All spaces already have a inbuilt order and function. There is a natural flow and quality of energy to each part of a space. Once a conscious living and working with energy begins to reveal this, it is simply a matter of allowing the process to unfold by continuing to develop good practices and persistently changing things to keep the process flowing – like stripping away layers to reveal the underlying core.

As the space becomes clearer, it will begin to resonate at a different level. Here the real business of tracking begins: watching a space change and moving with that change. For example, a space that you feel has always been very slow and stuck gradually becomes livelier and needs the new energy to be directed in a particular way. Or a space that needed fire and warmth to ignite its energy now needs grounding and stability.

This is sometimes the reason why, as soon as we have rearranged a room, we decide it needs redecorating, or we notice that we need to close off a doorway, and then we decide upon a ritual space clearing with lots of chanting. At each stage the space may feel perfect for a short time, and then we think of a way that will make it even better or closer to its natural order.

Have you ever painted a wall to find that as the colour goes on the whole room relaxes, as though it heaved a sigh of relief? Or have you ever stood back from a freshly painted wall and decided it should always have been that colour? When this begins to happen, the space is becoming so finely tuned that any further changes in the immediate future will be increasingly tiny ones.

HEALING THE LAND

Imagine being able to create this effect when working with buildings and land, even when their true nature has been obscured by a traumatic event or centuries of long-term abuse. Being able to help a space become energetically clearer is one thing – following that through and working to tune and fine-tune it is another.

By learning to work with the chi of a space, using your own chi with intent, breath, movement and sound, you can learn how to bring about this fine-tuning. This is the way energy workers, or shamans, have cleared and tuned large areas of space and the interiors of buildings, for centuries. These are the same techniques as those used to cleanse sites and allow them to move on to different functions, such as when rebuilding takes place on a piece of land, or a profane site is transformed into, or revealed to be, a sacred place.

BELOW **As you learn to work with energies according to the principles of Feng Shui, you will develop more accurate ideas about about how buildings affect a landscape. For example, the tall** chimneys below reflect rising wood energy, but they may be damaging the atmosphere. Power stations need to be designed very carefully in order to keep the area free from energetic pollution.

LEFT **Changes occur in the atmosphere of rooms that have been cleared of energy blockages. However, it may be necessary to** keep making adjustments in order to keep up with shifts in energy, perhaps by adding a vase of flowers or rearranging furniture.

5

tuning
your
space

TOP
10 QUESTIONS

調節空間

I have just moved into a new house where the previous occupants were really happy and have moved on to better things. Do I still need to space clear?

Yes, you still need to space clear, because even the happiest people leave energetic debris behind. Make it a gift to the house, rather like a first greeting to it.

I really enjoy space clearing and tuning, but I am not always sure when I have done enough and can stop work. How do I know when the work is completed?

There is no set rule for this. I would simply ask you how do you know when to finish eating or when to come inside after working in the garden? Work until you feel you have done enough, and be guided by the time and energy you have available.

I have been to see a house that all the locals say is haunted, and it felt spooky to me. I fell in love with it though. Should I buy it?

Why not? You seem to have been attracted to the house for a reason, and any energetic extras that come in the price can be a huge learning curve for you. There is no reason to believe that the rumours are true, it may just need a series of good space clears.

A friend has invited me to help her work on her space. Should I do it?

There is no reason why you shouldn't go along. Tune in with the space before you go, but keep an open mind until you arrive. Take a few of your tools with you. Be diligent with preparation and cleansing afterwards, and take a change of clothes and your own towel with you.

I try to set a time limit for space clearing, but sometimes it doesn't feel right to do this. Should I carry on at these times?

It does not matter if you get it wrong. You may have packed up, only to get the feeling that things are not done. You can go back to it there and then, or at a later stage. If you choose another time, write the time on a piece of paper and leave it in the space.

Are some places so bad energetically that they can never be clear?

Places are neither good nor bad. Some just need more careful work than others. I have never come across a space that could not be cleared and tuned, although some spaces have been so damaged that they can take considerable care, attention and love before they heal.

How can I get my cynical family to help space clear our house?

Have a party. Choose a day that feels auspicious (not someone's birthday). Clean the house and get everyone involved. Start the party at midday or dusk. Decorate the house with candles in winter or balloons in summer. Partying will enliven the energy: have champagne, and a cake with candles so you can make wishes.

調節空間

Can I use these techniques to work on my garden?

Absolutely. Outdoor spaces respond just as well to clearing, and even better to tuning. Some people get land cleared and tuned before starting work on a new building, and professional energy workers often work on land and in buildings that have changed use, for example when a hospital becomes a school.

How can I stop feeling tired or slightly ill after space clearing?

This is not unusual. I always rest after a big clearing job. Some work has the opposite effect and is invigorating. If you feel ill, clear yourself by drinking only water while you work and keep yourself warm. Waft incense, such as a smudge stick, around yourself afterwards to cleanse your aura.

When I am space clearing, is there a risk of making the energy worse instead of better? Should I only do it when I am feeling happy?

It is best only to work when you are feeling positive. Remember that like attracts like, so a negative, depressed mood will attract the wrong kind of energy into your space.

6

basic rules
for the
workplace

There are no real rules in Feng Shui for matching activities to spaces. A cramped cupboard-sized office may be a nightmare location for a musician struggling to write a symphony, but for the businessman who has 24 hours to complete his tax returns, and very limited powers of concentration, it could be perfect.

If you have a large, open-plan workplace with a wall of enormous windows and doors opening on to the garden, it probably seems ideal, until you discover that none of the sales you thought you had made have come to fruition, or at any rate, nobody has paid for the product. The wonderfully dispersed energy proved to be perfect for letting the world know how good your work was, but was of no help when it came to concluding the process and getting paid. For that you would need to find a quieter recess, with a round table on a dense square rug, and maybe a copper bowl and a vase of lilies.

Once again the whole thing becomes a matter of assessing the quality of energy in a space and proceeding from there. You always have the basic structure of Yin and Yang and the five elements to support you. Although there are no strict rules, the following guidelines may prove useful.

BELOW **T**he room below could serve as a primary school classroom where both teacher and students are very active. Decorations here are functional and movable, while there is a lot of space to add or take away materials and objects of study.

Yellow is good for mental stimulation

Semi-circular arrangement promotes interaction between pupils

Teacher's desk well placed for view of room

LEFT **I**n this classroom scene, pupils are obscuring each other's view of the teacher. It is important that furniture is arranged so that the pupils can interact with each other comfortably and have a good view of the teacher at the same time.

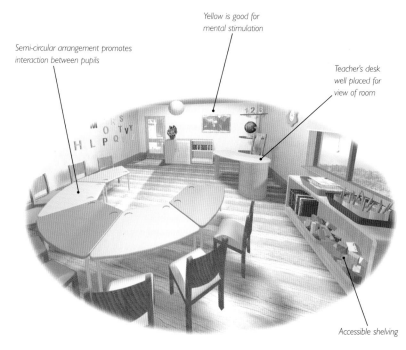

Accessible shelving

I consider a room without a window to be unfit for human habitation of any sort, work or otherwise. This means that all those basement workplaces and spaces sealed from the outside world are no-go areas. The excuses for using these rooms, such as the need for absolute darkness, silence or privacy, are not enough. All rooms need to be refreshed and revived with good quality air and daylight, even if only when work is over for the day. Given the availability of alternative accommodation in the building, nobody should be made to to work in a totally windowless space.

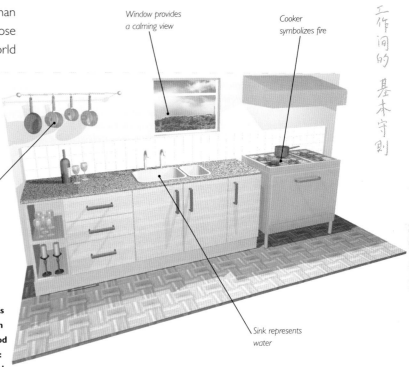

Window provides a calming view

Cooker symbolizes fire

工作间的 基本守则

Knives replaced with pans

Sink represents water

LEFT **This kitchen has not been arranged in accordance with good Feng Shui principles: fire and water should never be placed together, and the knives are not in an auspicious position. Arguments are likely to break out.**

ABOVE **In this kitchen, the furniture has been rearranged so that the cooker and the sink, which represent fire** **and water, are kept separate. The knives have also been removed from the wall and stored in a drawer.**

You must also take note of other features in a potential workspace. Work of any duration longer than a few minutes cannot usefully take place while sitting underneath a beam or the sharp angle of a sloping ceiling. These features cause the quality of the energy raining down on the worker's head to be very poor, which will affect his or her whole being. You may survive a working week sitting immediately under a low beam, but at what cost? But if such a location feels comfortable to you, I would recommend that you seriously consider the levels of stress that you have become used to, or maybe even addicted to, in other parts of your life and ask what role they play in maintaining you as the person you are.

Working in a space where a great catastrophe has occurred, and which has not been cleared energetically since that time, is simply asking for trouble. Trying to create something that will be the source of our income or recreation should not be done in a space that has recently been the site of degenerating energy.

If you lack confidence in a space in any way, or if you are ashamed of it, you should not work there. Work undertaken in such adverse conditions is unnecessarily stressful and will take its toll. If you consider that the energy of your surroundings is affecting you, and therefore your work, giving yourself a wonderful work environment should become part of your responsibility, not only to yourself, but to others.

NON-OFFICE WORKSPACES

A lot of work done from home takes place in an office set-up, but it also takes place in other surroundings. Whether you are setting up a studio for painting or sculpting, a kitchen for running a catering company, or a garden for growing and selling herbs, you can use some basic Feng Shui to help you improve your workspace. Once you have chosen your space with great care, you need to set boundaries. This means that if you are a cook, for example, you will need to keep the food you sell in a different place to the food you use for your family or yourself. Purchase a separate set of utensils for your business and store them separately from the ones you use to prepare your own food.

If you run a gardening business, do not be tempted to squeeze some of the plants destined for sale in amongst your perennial border: grow them in a different bed, or keep the plant pots on a separate shelf in the greenhouse.

Aim to separate office and home telephone and fax lines. If you have clients coming to your home, bring them in through a different door to the one the family uses if possible, and restrict their access to the house. Make provisions for them in your workspace: a comfortable chair or coffee-making facility may be all that is needed to prevent you from having to resort to your home space.

Therapists and healers working from home need to be absolutely meticulous in setting up and maintaining boundaries between work and home, always aiming to have separate toilet facilities, entrances and passageways for clients.

Even if limited space does not enable you to achieve these aims, conscious use of existing space and esoteric demarcations will help.

Commercial plants kept separate

Path separates business and domestic activities, but should be curved

Curving hedge allows chi to flow gently

Fence provides a boundary

LEFT **B**oundaries must be set for different activities that take place in the same area. For example, a gardener who wishes to sell seeds and plants from his own garden, must keep items for sale in a separate area to avoid confusion.

BELOW **G**ardens need a sense of order and structure, especially when they are used as a place of business.

A curved fence would be better here; the energy created would help the gardener reap the rewards of hard work.

工作间的 基本守则

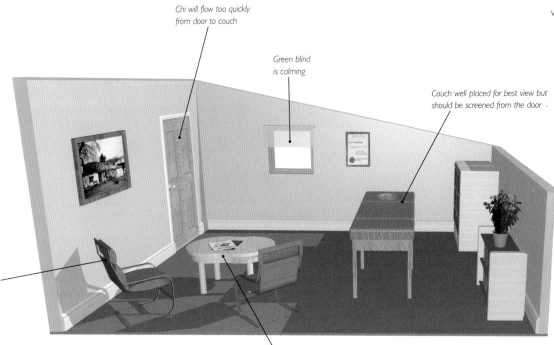

RIGHT **The therapist's couch in this room has been moved out of the way of the sloping ceiling, and repositioned so that the patient has a clear view of the door and the window. This will help the patient to feel safe and comfortable.**

Chi will flow too quickly from door to couch

Green blind is calming

Couch well placed for best view but should be screened from the door

Good position for therapist's view of door and couch

Chi will flow gently around table's curves

Once you have established boundaries, in time as well as space, walk into your room – while it is still empty if possible – and decide where you would work best. This will involve taking some time to walk around and sit or stand in various locations. If your job involves several different tasks, choose the ideal space for each task. You can then set boundaries, and position the furniture, equipment and tools within these areas.

It is important to be aware of the position of windows and doors, and the placement of sloping ceilings, beams, recesses and alcoves. Working with your back towards the door can be stressful, so avoid this position. Move power points and heat sources so they are more convenient: so many people work in locations made miserable by poorly sited amenities, because they do not feel they can justify the cost or effort involved in moving a power point or a telephone line. If you work from home, give yourself the best of everything so that you can get the best out of yourself.

BELOW **This therapist's room does not display good Feng Shui. The couch is under the sloping ceiling, and positioned so that the patient cannot see the door or the window. In addition, the red curtains are not relaxing and will create a tense atmosphere.**

WORKING FROM HOME

The arrival of modern technology has enabled a greater number of people to work from home nowadays, but we need to readdress the way we arrange our space to accommodate the extra activity. It is not enough simply to turn a spare room into a workspace and expect all to be well. I have often seen people do this, only to find that the quality of their work begins to suffer, their work is less in demand, or that they simply lose all incentive to work and all joy in the process. There may also be unexpected and unwanted repercussions in their home lives.

Very often the nature of a person's work introduces an entirely new set of connections into the home. For example, taking a difficult business call in the kitchen while your husband cooks supper is the modern-day equivalent of wearing a pair of muddy farm boots and tramping right the way through the house. The energy of the phone call gets cooked right into the food and the whole family can end up feeling harassed and belligerent by the end of the meal.

Using a room simply because it is available or can be spared is no place from which to produce any service or product that is going to be highly valued in the marketplace. Taking over a prime living space is no guarantee for success either; a good master bedroom is rarely a good office.

IMPLICATIONS

When you are considering working from home, the most important thing is to be clear about the nature of the work you are intending to do, and to consider how it will affect the space, and how the space may affect the work. For example, a house that has been chosen as (and designed purely around) a place for leisure and relaxation, may be an ideal site for a sport and fitness company, but not for use as a solicitor's office. A busy house full of noisy children and dogs may be an excellent place to sell cookers, but not so good for sitting quietly and designing bedlinen. Work activity should support the energy in the home, while the home should support the workspace.

BELOW **It is not a good idea to position your workspace below a sloping roof or flight of stairs. The energy will be oppressive and will not be conducive to creative thinking.**

工作间的 基本守则

Chair should have
good view of window

Inspiring view will
help imagination

Picture of landscape
is uplifting

Chair base should
be more secure

BELOW **A Yang room in
a very active, noisy
household would not
be a suitable place for
any activity requiring
focused concentration
and contemplation.**

ABOVE **The place where
you decide to work
must be appropriate
for the nature of your
business. For example,
the isolation and**
**bareness of this room
would be ideal for
completing tasks, but
an unsuitable venue for
meeting and
entertaining clients.**

MATCHING THE FIVE ELEMENTS TO ACTIVITIES

It is often fairly obvious how activities and spaces match or mismatch. The five elements *(see page 21)* can also help here, because each activity is associated with an element and you can apply its considerations. Thinking in terms of the blend of capabilities and qualities you use in your job will help you to select the appropriate space for your workplace, and design it in a supportive way. Here are some examples of activities and their related elements.

WOOD

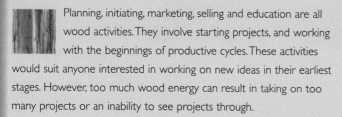

Planning, initiating, marketing, selling and education are all wood activities. They involve starting projects, and working with the beginnings of productive cycles. These activities would suit anyone interested in working on new ideas in their earliest stages. However, too much wood energy can result in taking on too many projects or an inability to see projects through.

FIRE

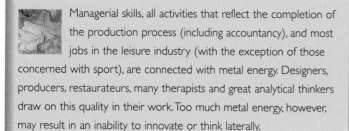

Sport, leisure, media and public relations are associated with fire energy. These careers involve being active and in the public eye. They are high-energy, volatile professions, and would also include anyone who wishes to pursue a career in the entertainment industry. An excess of fire energy can lead to 'burn out' and exhaustion.

METAL

Managerial skills, all activities that reflect the completion of the production process (including accountancy), and most jobs in the leisure industry (with the exception of those concerned with sport), are connected with metal energy. Designers, producers, restaurateurs, many therapists and great analytical thinkers draw on this quality in their work. Too much metal energy, however, may result in an inability to innovate or think laterally.

EARTH

The service industry (including the caring professions – doctors, nurses, social workers, residential care home staff), food production, human resource management and work directly involved with using the earth's resources, such as mining, are all associated with earth energy. These are activities that rely on an ability to use resources effectively, whilst remaining centred and self-possessed. The jobs span a huge range of abilities and talents. These are also professions that can take in raw materials and transform and output them without any loss of rhythm or capability. Too much earth energy can cause a cluttered lifestyle, however, with a tendency to keep too many objects for a 'rainy day'.

WATER

Artists, poets, writers, philosophers, some therapists and healers are all engaged in water activity. These are professions that call upon an ability to harness deep resources from within in order to work intuitively, or to express vision and creativity, whilst still retaining a quality of stillness. This contemplative side also gives birth to inventiveness of every description, including scientific breakthroughs. Innovation and ground-breaking new ideas will be the result of positive water energy; however if there is an excess of water chi it can lead to daydreaming or depression.

Good position for chair

Round table is
good for meetings

Accessible storage

High-backed
chairs give a
secure feeling

LEFT **T**his room would be suitable for a restless travel agent who finds it difficult to settle down to work. The round table will encourage completion of tasks, and the high-backed chairs will help the occupant to start new projects.

WORKING WITH THE ELEMENTS

Imagine you want to create a space for finishing the design of a CD cover. Creativity and completion are both supported by metal energy, so an uncluttered space with clean lines would be a good place to choose. Look for a room facing west or south-west, preferably one with a good view, with some interesting detail in the middle distance. This will support creativity without encouraging a tendency to daydream. You should light a candle to encourage a bit of action and move the phone out until the project is complete, or until you are ready to book in some more work.

Someone setting up a company to sell holidays would need a well organized room with a high-backed chair and a rounded desk. If getting down to work proved to be difficult, the chair would have to be moved to where there was a clear view of both a window and the door, with support behind it from a wall or a strong piece of furniture. The high-backed chair and well organized room boost wood energy, which is associated with the ability to initiate projects and think ahead. The rounded desk promotes metal energy, enabling deals to be clinched and success in the travel industry to be achieved. The location of the chair will boost the person's power base and promote clear thoughts and forward vision.

BELOW **T**his room would suit a creative writer or designer who requires an uncluttered and harmonious workspace with clean lines, a window with a beautiful, uplifting view, a candle to encourage activity, and no telephone to disturb concentration.

BELOW **O**pen-plan offices make it difficult to follow the rules of Feng Shui. However, you can do things to free blocked chi and to improve your working environment, such as tackling the position of your desk and chair.

RIGHT **H**anging a heavy, protective jacket on the back of your chair gives you the tortoise energy your placement in an office may lack. You can also improve the clarity of your phoenix energy by clearing your desk, keeping on it only things that are in constant use.

OPEN-PLAN OFFICES AND 'HOT DESKING'

Even if your workplace is not in the home, correct Feng Shui is just as important. If you have your own clearly defined and separate space, you can utilize some of the techniques you have been using at home to improve your working environment. For example, it is often reasonably easy for a teacher with a fixed classroom, or people with their own room or office, to transform the energy there. However, many people find it more of a problem when they work in an open-plan environment, or if they have to move to different locations throughout the day.

The most important thing you can take to work to improve the Feng Shui of your workplace is your attitude. A heightened awareness of the dynamics of the space is the best Feng Shui cure of all.

Look first at the place in which you spend most of your time. If you are fairly stationary, it is important that you pay some attention to getting that place right. If you move about during the day, you need to consider the quality of chi in the wider environment. If you sit at a desk in an open-plan office, look carefully at the position of your chair with regard to the window and door. Try to create a protected position for your back and an open space in front of you. Pay attention to how the chi flows around where you sit and, if you feel hemmed in, try to open things up.

Now look at your tortoise and phoenix energy. If it is lacking, and you cannot move your desk to compensate, you can increase the clarity in front of you by keeping your desk absolutely clear and storing anything that is not in constant use. Create support at the back by repositioning your chair, or changing it for one with a stronger, higher back in a more striking colour. Alternatively, use that wonderfully mobile Feng Shui cure loved by consultants everywhere: the heavy protective jacket hung on the back of the chair. At all costs avoid sitting with your back to a walkway, or at the end of the corridor with people walking towards you all day.

If your work position stops you from seeing who is approaching you, a small angled mirror will remedy the situation. If you have to share desks or workstations (so-called 'hot desking'), take your remedies with you and set them up wherever you are working.

CHECKING THE ENERGY FLOW

If life at work is hard, look at what is in your immediate environment. Change a spiky cactus for a softer plant, or a drooping plant for an uplifting specimen. Move to face away from a brick wall or at least put a huge picture of a sea or landscape on it. Otherwise, check to see who is sitting immediately in front of you in the chi flow of the room. Remember, chi moves in through the door and clockwise (in the northern hemisphere) around the room, therefore the person who is in the position before you in the chi flow will be having an effect on you. Also, if you have to change desks regularly, consider who was using a desk before you, because you will be picking up on his or her energy.

USING A PORTABLE FENG SHUI KIT

Put together a portable kit containing objects that are meaningful to you, such as a candle, a small bowl for water or essential oils, a photograph of someone who loves you, or a card with an inspiring message. Use it to improve your space. Once you nurture a small area around you, other people may join in and a slow transformation results. If nothing else is possible, buy yourself a mug you really like, or start taking good quality drinking water and a cut-glass tumbler to work. Fresh flowers work wonders because of the combinations of shapes, colours and aromas you can introduce, and because you can add glass and water before choosing a perfect location for them.

When good Feng Shui principles are set to work in a large office building, conflict and sickness can be made a thing of the past, and creativity and productivity allowed to flourish. Slight adjustments, such as a few people swapping desks or changing partitions, can make a big difference and, if people are prepared to change offices with one another, or add plants or new touches of colour, the transformation can be remarkable. For example, it is no use siting a managing director's office on the ground floor of a ten-floor office complex. Although she is the most powerful member of the company, her abilities are inhibited by this location. Correct Feng Shui will allow her to do her job properly.

Feng Shui can release the true potential of a workplace, and create a happier, more harmonious working environment.

ABOVE **Feng Shui can be invaluable to a business by helping it to rearrange its offices to ensure that the correct activities take place in the most suitable areas of the building. For example, the leaders of the company should have offices on higher floors and be supported on the lower floors by middle management.**

BELOW **Personal touches – like a potted plant, a photograph of someone you love or a special coffee cup – can improve the energy of your working area.**

6

basic rules for the workplace

TOP 10 QUESTIONS

調
節
空
間

Which plants are best for offices?

Only those plants that are well cared for and enjoyed regularly. Spiky plants are better off in the open spaces of their natural habitat than on your desk. Assess a plant for shape and energy: does it flow, droop, grow like a bush, shoot up towards the sky, or parade its finery? Once you know this, you can link it to one of the five elements (see page 21).

There is not much natural light in my workspace. What can I do?

If you need a lot of light, consider moving. If your only choice is to boost existing light levels, choose pale, warm colours with silky or shiny finishes to reflect light. Move large, dark furniture away from light sources, or remove it altogether. Add pictures full of light, framed in reflective materials, and add glass to increase the light levels.

How can I store the things I need for my job in accordance with good Feng Shui rules?

Clear any clutter, and position remaining objects in accordance with their energy. Store files behind you to increase tortoise energy. Put new projects, ideas marketing and sales to your left. Place accounts, invoices and administration to your right. Finally, keep the phoenix area in front of you as clear as you can.

Are some desk shapes better than others?

The shape and colour of your desk is very important. A large, solid, black desk is excellent for finance, a rectangular desk made from a light-coloured wood will be good for new ventures, while a desk with a gentler shape and colour – for example, a curved desk painted dove grey – will support creativity.

工作间的 基本守则

I have created a workspace in my garden shed. What can I do to improve its Feng Shui?

Treat it like any other building. Clean and decorate it with love, space clear and tune it, and arrange furniture with care. Ensure it has good tortoise, dragon, tiger and phoenix energy. Ask yourself, though, if being a 'satellite' is a problem for you or a role you enjoy.

I am a hairdresser, and I visit customers in their homes. What should I do to make the right Feng Shui improvements?

Your most powerful allies will be the products you use. Try to use natural products, free from chemical additives and smells, to keep your clients healthy and reduce your stress levels. Also keep the use of hairdryers to a minimum.

I run a sales office and I am about to order some new office furniture. Which shapes and materials would you suggest?

Avoid anything that will make you too relaxed, like flowing blues and violets. Use lively greens with touches of bright flame colours. Add a few shiny textures combined with denser materials for floors and seating.

I work in a shop all day serving customers. How can I improve my Feng Shui?

This is one of those cases where Feng Shui is not a realistic option. If it is your own shop, of course, things could be different, but if you are employed to move around the shop all day, there is little you can do except gently make the owner aware of Feng Shui!

In order to avoid cluttering up my workspace, I have stored as many files as possible on my computer, but is it possible to have electronic clutter?

This is one of the most common forms of hidden clutter. Have a regular clear out at least once every three months, and do not be tempted to file every document.

I have heard that sitting too near to electrical appliances has a negative effect. I have many appliances in my office, including a computer, desk lamp, palmtop organizer, a telephone, and a digital clock. Do I need to worry?

No, but remove the things you can, like the digital clock. Add plants to the sides and rear of remaining equipment. Wear natural fabrics, and wash them daily.

7

feng shui
and other
people

iving alone, a thing that in some societies would be seen as a great hardship, has today become the chosen lifestyle for many people. Given our current emphasis on individual achievement, living alone is the natural progression for many people who need a space that is within their control and a reflection of their own needs, talents and lifestyle.

Living alone allows a person to change and grow in ways that would be almost impossible under the constraints of a partnership or group. If you are lucky enough to be able to choose your own personal space, you give yourself the opportunity of creating an environment that will become a never-ending gift.

If you find yourself in a space that was originally for a partnership or group, it is important to close off that stage of its existence and recreate it in a way that is an expression of your own needs. This will involve a thorough clearing of clutter, and a generic space clear and tune. You will also need to rededicate the space to allow your new beginning. Creating a habitable space for one person can be very exciting, but it is necessary to begin the process of creating (or recreating) the space from a position of strength and positivity.

CONNECTING WITH YOUR SPACE

Imagine a place that makes you to feel exhilarated, centred and alive, and use it to inspire your creation of your own space. Try to find a place like it in real life. If it is within easy travelling distance, go there.

BELOW **The best thing that you can do is to live in an environment that makes you feel inspired and that never stops giving something to you – it should be somewhere that enables you to create the kind of life you wish to live.**

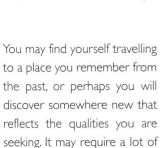

RIGHT **If you find that your idea of a perfect place is sitting with your back to a tree, note your need for tortoise energy, and seek out the features in your environment that will give you the support and safety that you need.**

You may find yourself travelling to a place you remember from the past, or perhaps you will discover somewhere new that reflects the qualities you are seeking. It may require a lot of research before you find your perfect place, which could turn out to be a cliff-top, or even a bench at the city mall. Once you have found this place, it will be easier to realize the spatial qualities you need in your new home.

Needless to say, everyone is different. Some people want a wide open space, wind and sun; others prefer the deep energy of a café under a railway embankment. If you have not been able to find an actual space that matches the one in your mind's eye, continue to visualize it instead.

Whether your perfect place is real or imagined, sit down in it – or visualize yourself sitting down in it – and become aware of the qualities of that space all around you, including those above and below, and the distant ones as well as those nearby. Recognize which features of the place make you feel good. Once you are certain about these features make a list of them, and add to your list the compass direction you have chosen to face, and any other spatial details. Note the colours, shapes and textures you like, and the features that give you a feeling of exhilaration. Write down everything you notice – we are apt to overlook the important ones that are difficult to achieve – but it is essential to include them. Then examine

your list – it may surprise you. Now you will have a better idea of what kind of environment makes you feel good. From this moment on, creating your space will be a source of joy, because the main themes of your space are now in position. For example, if you wrote 'carpet of flowers' on your list, you should spend extra money on your flooring because it matters to you. If you found yourself sitting in a crowded bar in the centre of town, on a seat by the window with a view of the street, you can throw away any details of country houses and start looking at apartments in town.

On a subtler level, look at how you positioned yourself in your chosen space, and what you put high on your list of desirable features. If you sat with your back to a tree, do not compromise on the tortoise energy of your space. If you chose a beach but you really liked the towering cliffs at the side, then take that into account. You may have chosen a place because it made you feel safe, or one that let you feel you could breathe. Make sure the home you choose enables you to feel those things.

When you have reviewed your list, choose four items that you will not compromise over. Remember that you are not trying to recreate your ideal place, but simply trying to discover the energetic and spatial qualities that work for you. Finally, if you are not enjoying making a space for one, maybe what you really need to be doing is creating a space to share.

LIVING AS A COUPLE

Sharing is the key word here. If one person dominates a space, he or she will be squeezing out the other person in many ways. The home will, in effect, only be serving the needs of one person.

I once visited a couple who were living in a huge house, where the husband only had a downstairs cloakroom to call his own. I have been in spaces so packed full of one person's possessions that calling it shared space was a travesty.

Living together involves finding a point of balance that is acceptable to you both. If you live with a partner, you can use your space to diagnose what is happening in the relationship, to build on the good things and sort out the bad. What were your expectations of the space when you first decided on it, and when you subsequently moved in? Did you both choose the space together, or did one person originally live in it, and the other one moved in later? Examining the original motives for choosing your space will help you to work out how your expectations of it have affected your relationship to each other.

Go through the space, interpreting it as a direct reflection of the state of your relationship. For example, lots of things begun but left unfinished will tell you to slow down and give each other more time; one person's clutter clogging up mutual space will suggest it is time for the clutter-fiend to deal with some personal issues and to give the other person, and the relationship, a little more room. A wonderfully appointed living room and hallway alongside a down-at-heel bedroom and bathroom, suggest that the appearance of a successful relationship may disguise underlying difficulties.

The process of discovery should lead to some realizations and opportunities to move forward and redesign the space. If you get stuck at a discussion, or conflict, stage during this process, there is nothing like a little practical Feng Shui to get things moving. Try rearranging some items and see how you feel, or start by doing the things you both find acceptable and see what happens. No one needs to feel pressurized. Remember, some of us may be working through a lot of damage from past relationships. We can find ways to help each other change without triggering old responses. How about indulging each other with a little love and humour?

BELOW **A couple must allow each other equal space in a shared home. This sitting room indicates an interest in music. If this is the hobby of only one person, he or she is letting it dominate the relationship.**

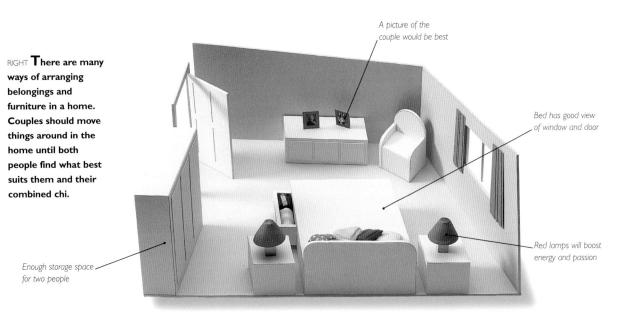

RIGHT **There are many ways of arranging belongings and furniture in a home. Couples should move things around in the home until both people find what best suits them and their combined chi.**

A picture of the couple would be best

Bed has good view of window and door

Red lamps will boost energy and passion

Enough storage space for two people

SUPPORT AND EMPOWERMENT

A good indication of how things really are for a couple can be found by making a Feng Shui assessment of the bedroom. I did a consultation for a couple who were living in a beautiful apartment with their five children. Things had become a bit of a struggle for the pair, in spite of a lot of support and help in the running of the family and the day-to-day affairs.

One look at the master bedroom told me exactly where things were going wrong. The well-intentioned couple had given the children the best and most energetically powerful rooms, and contented themselves with a relatively small, dull room slightly apart from the rest of the house. They were therefore sacrificing their quality of life for that of their children. The children were thriving, if a bit too headstrong, but the parents were in danger of splitting up, and were only just managing to keep the family together.

I suggested that the parents take on the most powerful room in the apartment and move the eldest child, who needed to separate and move on, to a small room by the front door. Entranced by this increase in his freedom and independence, the eldest child was delighted to swap, while the parents moved into a position that not only supported them as a couple, but also empowered them to guide the family.

ABOVE **Humour and a little indulgence of the other person goes a long way in working out problems** between partners, but the shared home, or a particular room and its contents, could also need changing.

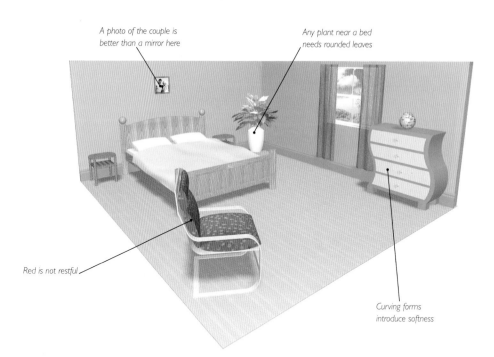

A photo of the couple is
better than a mirror here

Any plant near a bed
needs rounded leaves

Red is not restful

Curving forms
introduce softness

CREATING A BEDROOM FOR TWO

Not only the choice of bedroom, but its design, layout and usage will tell you how you can enhance your relationship. Take a long look at the room. Look at the colours you have chosen to have around you, and the sorts of things you have in the room. If you have chosen cool blues, you may wonder why you spend so much time alone in your room thinking; if the room is white, you may find it difficult to relax. Refer back to the elements and their corresponding colours (see page 21) and you will see why red is associated with passion. Warm earth colours are good for closeness; green is enlivening, and red will keep you awake all night. Consider opting for blends of colour, or combinations with accessories to add a spark.

The layout of furniture is important. Aim for balance and flow with a few details to liven things up. For example, two bedside tables, a solid mahogany bed with a beautiful curving headboard, and a chest of drawers built from antique wood could be balanced with a lightweight wicker chair and another more frivolous piece. Big pieces of heavy furniture reflect commitment and stability, but too much can mean lack of lightheartedness and fun. If the overall feel of the room is of softness and femininity, perhaps you need to introduce

ABOVE **W**arm earth colours encourage closeness and stability, but the mirror above the fireplace could create friction because of the excess of fire energy.

ABOVE **Y**our approach to sharing space in your home will reflect your true feelings towards your mate, and vice versa. **A bedroom that supports the two people who share it will make their home a foundation for them, so that they thrive as individuals while enjoying the security of a harmonious relationship.**

some hard edges and clean lines to add Yang and improve the overall balance of the room.

Notice how Yin and Yang qualities work together in the room, looking always to create movement and fun against a backdrop of commitment and safety.

Lack of passion in a relationship is very often a symptom, not a cause, of a problem. You would be advised to look beyond the bedroom for signs of repression or resentment, rather than rush out to buy a pair of red candles and hope all will be well.

If you really want to share your life and yourself with your partner, you will find this reflected in your approach to your living space. Harboured meanness or a lack of trust will find expression in selfishly guarded treasures or areas that no one else is allowed to touch. These give the wrong messages to your partner.

A space that is created and loved by two people will allow the relationship to grow and let the couple enjoy a real sense of freedom within the context of commitment and harmony.

CREATING SPACE FOR A BABY

If your baby is born at home, you will quickly realize how the event has transformed the energy of the whole living space. The simple fact of having a baby living in the home wakes up the chi and gives us a chance to see things more clearly.

While your baby shares your sleeping area, allow the energy to flow and grow a little more earthy. To do this, let things accumulate at ground level and use gentle colours such as dull gold, dusky pink, pale apricot or muted green. Let muffling textures such as crushed velvet or lambswool slow the room's energy, and put rag rugs or sisal on the floor. Leave sudden changes and bright colours for another time, draw back the curtains a little later in the day, and do things at a gentle pace.

The room should become a point of centred peace and equilibrium. Even if the surroundings are loud with activity, keep this space a sanctuary of calm. Allow things to accumulate a little; the time for clearing was before the birth. Accept the decor as it is for a while. This is not a time to redesign or redecorate.

LEFT **When you share your bedroom with your baby, it is important to maintain the space as a sanctuary of calm and equilibrium. Babies need earth energy, so keep to soft and muted earth colours, and keep the light from windows as gentle as possible.**

BELOW **A** child will be unable to sleep well in this bed; its location between the wardrobes under the triangular structure will cause very poor development.

RIGHT **A**lthough blue is usually a relaxing colour, this room is too stimulating for a baby. The birds and the cascading curtains add to the 'busy' atmosphere. It would be better to simplify the curtains with subdued tones, and tone down the walls.

MOVING A BABY TO A SEPARATE ROOM

Once the time has come for the baby to move out of your room, make sure it is a gradual process. Start by feeding your child in the new space, so that your baby's first impression of the place is one of contentment. Gradually build up the happy time you spend there, and leave nappy changes to happen elsewhere. When the time comes for your baby to sleep in that room, he or she will accept the space as a good place to be.

For an easy transition, aim to blend the feeling of the old room with the new. You could move a chair from your room into the baby's room, for example, or any other items that smell and feel familiar.

It is best to set up the space well before the move, especially if you are decorating, because the smell of new paint will aggravate your child. When thinking of the room's layout and design, you need to be very aware of its location and shape. Avoid a room with a door opening directly on to the top of the stairs, or one that is directly opposite the bathroom. Babies need quiet, slow energy in a bedroom; they have enough happening in their own little worlds without needing any extra stimulation. They are also very sensitive to the kinds of energy imbalance we have learnt to screen out of conscious awareness, so your baby would be better off staying with you than being put to sleep in a room at the end of the hall with sloping ceilings and a skylight.

DECORATING YOUR CHILD'S ROOM

A small child needs a well-proportioned room with adequate light. Choose gentle colours that blend and tone, such as pastel blue to calm and steady the energy, pink for gentle stimulation and warmth, soft yellow to nourish and support, and pale green to enliven the atmosphere a little. There is no need to use primary colours, bold designs and jagged edges to stimulate them. Many parents decorate their baby's room with an array of strident colours, pictures and toys and then wonder why the child sleeps fitfully, cannot settle and needs constant attention. Babies need lots of earth energy. Take the energy of the room down to the floor, with layers of natural textures that they can explore once they are mobile. Choose low, squat furniture with soft, rounded edges, and natural fabrics.

KEEPING THINGS SIMPLE AND SAFE

Try to maintain an atmosphere of simplicity and clarity in your child's room. There is no reason to dangle lots of things from the ceiling – a few beautiful shapes, maybe a hanging spiral of colour, is enough. Strong roots in the home will enable your baby to grow and develop; properly grounded, babies will progress rapidly.

Take care with the placement of the baby's bed. Keep the head of the bed away from a window, do not line up the foot with the door, and never put the bed under the slope of a ceiling. Also consider what is on the other side of the wall next to the bed (in the room next door). Make sure there is nothing that will create a strong electromagnetic field or be harmful to the baby, such as the back of a television set.

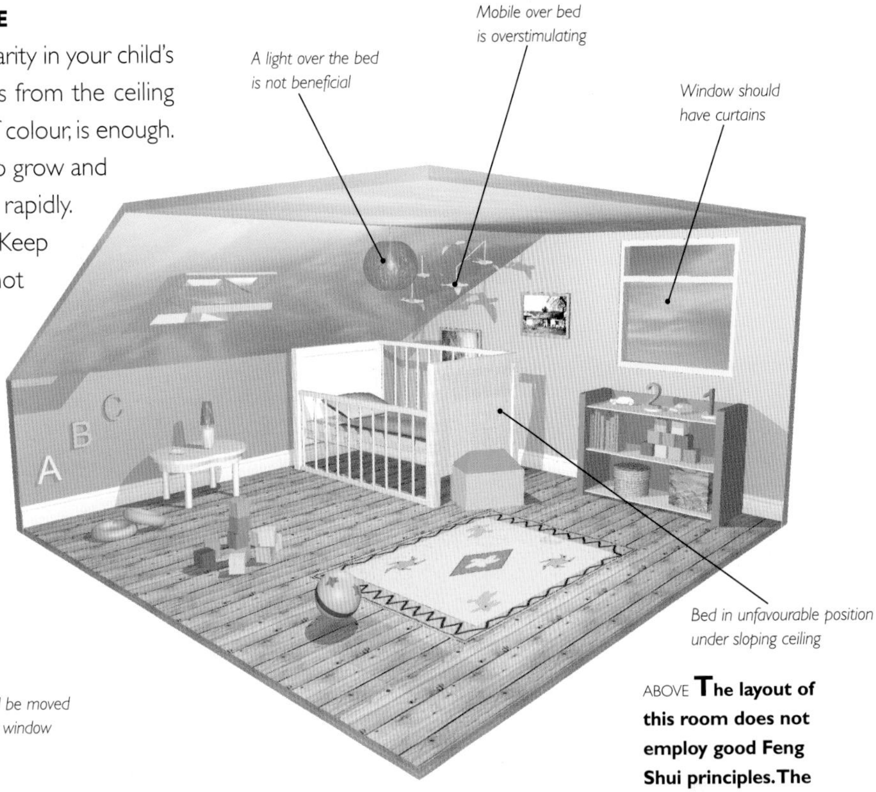

Mobile over bed is overstimulating

A light over the bed is not beneficial

Window should have curtains

Bed in unfavourable position under sloping ceiling

ABOVE **T**he layout of this room does not employ good Feng Shui principles. The bed is positioned under the sloping ceiling and almost under the skylight, and the mobile overhead is not restful.

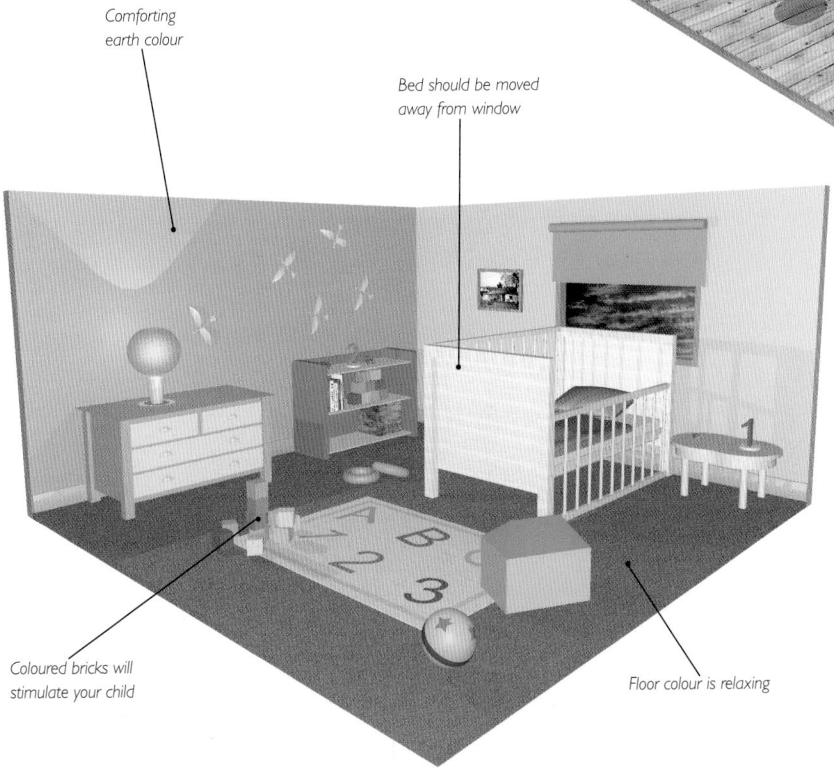

Comforting earth colour

Bed should be moved away from window

LEFT **T**he warm earth tones of these walls are relaxing and give the room an air of stability, but the child's bed should be moved because it is not good Feng Shui to place the bed under a window in this way.

Coloured bricks will stimulate your child

Floor colour is relaxing

RIGHT **Playful features in a child's room, like this fish-shaped coat rack, may also help him or her to learn how to be tidy.**

LEFT **Small chairs and other child-sized furnishings will help your children to feel comfortable and welcome in the home.**

RIGHT **Containers in which children can easily store their toys when they are finished with them are essential for bedrooms and playrooms.**

CREATING SPACE FOR OLDER CHILDREN

Sharing our space with a child or children can be very challenging. It is not enough to set aside a room for them, decorate it tastefully and expect life to continue as normal. We need to be much more generous, and learn to adapt to the changing needs of the family.

If a child is being difficult or causing anxiety, you should look at the way the space is being used. Have you given your children low-energy, water-type rooms to play in, but found that they are taking friends into your south-facing active areas instead? Are attention-craving children being asked to use rooms built in extensions, or with a bathroom between them and their siblings and parents?

Children do not just need space, they need appropriate space like anyone else. A demanding child needs space to sleep close to parents, and should play in integrated family space.

We need to make adjustments to the way we share our space with our children. Put a desk in the kitchen where a small child can set up camp and store toys and treasures. A box of toys for quiet play in the sitting room will keep children happy while you enjoy adult company. Children need boundaries, but if you let them integrate into your space, and not overrun it, then life will flow smoothly.

As they grow older, your children will gradually be able to move into their own space for longer periods of time. Giving them their own things right through the house will signal to them what you expect of them. Rooms with nothing for them to use will signal that they are spaces that you do not expect them to be in.

Give your children the means to grow and learn in a steady, practical way. Give them coathooks they can easily reach, put cups and drinks where they are accessible, keep a low stool by the sink so that they can stand on it to wash their hands, and buy them an apron so that they can see they should be involved in cooking and other tasks. These things will all signal to them what you expect them to be doing.

Likewise, an absence of paints and no television in their bedrooms will signal to your children that you do not expect them to be doing these things in their rooms. You lead the way, listening to their ideas and learning from them as you go. At the end of the day the responsibility for choosing designs and colours must be yours, but a little careful planning will make life run more smoothly.

SLOW CHILDREN

A slow, apathetic child will need a bright, roomy space with large windows covered with simple fabric. Splashes of green or red complement positive open designs on furnishings and bedlinen. If your child is unwell, consult a qualified Feng Shui practitioner before choosing a colour scheme for the room.

OVERACTIVE CHILDREN

An overactive child would be better placed in a small, cosy room to encourage less active play and help him or her to be calm. A thick, intricately designed rug will encourage precise inward play, and a wonderful view from the window will encourage imagination, and with it the love of creative and more directional play. Construction toys will harness your child's energy in a new way.

NERVOUS CHILDREN

A nervous child will need safety. Look beyond the bedroom door into the hall and find a place for a picture he or she will love, or a chest with some soft toys – anything that will indicate that the space is safe and protected. Choose warm earth tones for your child's room, and add gentle, layered window coverings such as delicately printed cotton and draped voile, arranged so that harsh window edges are softened. Check that the bed is well placed, and away from the door and windows.

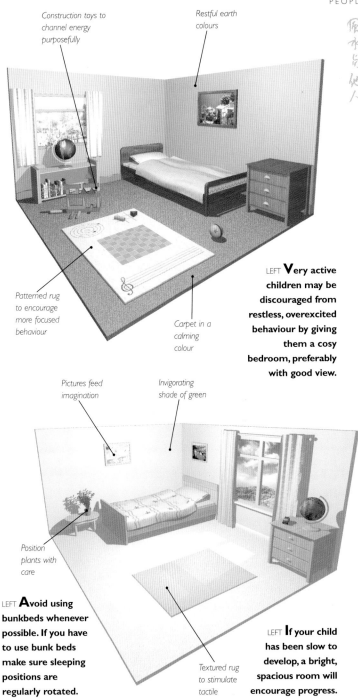

Construction toys to channel energy purposefully

Restful earth colours

Patterned rug to encourage more focused behaviour

Carpet in a calming colour

LEFT **Very active children may be discouraged from restless, overexcited behaviour by giving them a cosy bedroom, preferably with good view.**

Pictures feed imagination

Invigorating shade of green

Position plants with care

LEFT **Avoid using bunkbeds whenever possible. If you have to use bunk beds make sure sleeping positions are regularly rotated.**

Textured rug to stimulate tactile experience

LEFT **If your child has been slow to develop, a bright, spacious room will encourage progress.**

91

ABOVE **Parents should try to cater to teenagers' needs for the colour black, which helps them to turn inwards and explore themselves. Let them have black stereo equipment, black-painted furniture and black throws for chairs to satisfy this need.**

LIVING WITH TEENAGERS

The teenage years span a time of deep transformation. If your teenager appears to be changing rapidly on the outside, on the inside change is happening on a magnificent scale. So let us deal with the black bedroom scenario right at the beginning. The colour black takes our attention deep into ourselves; it feeds the absorption of profound change and awesome transformation. Your little bug is turning into a butterfly, soon to fly off alone. Teenagers need their black; maybe draw the line at black walls and curtains, but understand the desire and give your child a black throw for a chair, black paint to spray a bedside cabinet, and all the black stereo equipment your neighbourhood can handle!

Within this context, following their need for clues about how to negotiate this difficult time, adolescents sometimes search out bright reds or other garish colours that you may find grating. Some like to fill their rooms with candles and incense. Fire energy lights the way forward, and enables flashes of understanding. Just keep an eye on the safety aspect and make sure your child is aware of the dangers.

If we understand why these things are happening, it will help us to know how to deal with them. Loud music, for example, helps us to enter a dream state, a helpful place to be when learning how to deal with the difficulties of youth.

BELOW **A teenager may wish to rearrange his or her bedroom periodically. Feng Shui rules should not always be applied to this age group.**

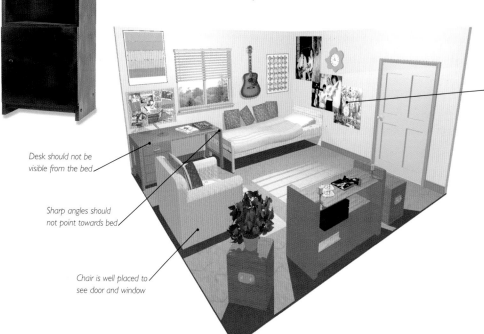

Desk should not be visible from the bed

Sharp angles should not point towards bed

Chair is well placed to see door and window

Allow freedom of choice in what goes on the walls

EXTENDING THE BOUNDARIES

Having understood that most of what teenagers do with their space is part of learning to cope with this stage in their lives, we should consider allowing them to arrange their space as they see fit, but within clearly defined boundaries.

Teenagers are usually at that point between needing to live in the family home and wanting to move on. If you allow your teenager's room to become the single person's apartment he or she would probably like, you may well remove the impetus to move. On the other hand, if you continue to interfere in the space, tidying, sorting and rearranging, you are depriving your teenager of the experience of creating a space, as he or she will need to do when the time does come to move on.

You need to draw boundaries for your son or daughter in respect of how they care for the space. Obviously, as your teenager grows older, the boundaries will change. For example, a teenager's room is often a place where a lot of socializing goes on, and sometimes becomes a real focal point. Give as much space and privacy as you possibly can. Help with arranging each area of the room in terms of function.

A teenager who is proving unable to cope with the freedom she is currently enjoying could be helped by a change of bedroom, perhaps to one closer to a younger sibling, or nearer her parents. Watch carefully if your son or daughter has recently moved into a room situated in a wing or extension of the house – he or she may not be quite ready to cope with this new-found freedom.

Teenagers, in my experience, are an example of a group that moves beyond a lot of what classical Feng Shui dictates. For example, for most people I would advise against en suite bathrooms or any water source in the bedroom. It is far healthier to keep all such arrangements away from normal living areas. I would usually advise against sleeping in rooms with sloping ceilings, or rooms with windows looking out on to walls or nearby trees. However, because of the unique nature of the teenage years it appears that, for short periods at least, all these spatial configurations are fine, or even desirable.

LEFT **Giving a teenager a certain amount of privacy and freedom to decorate and care for her own room will give her independence and help to prepare her for a more self-reliant future.**

7

feng shui and other people

TOP 10 QUESTIONS

My teenager treats our house like a hotel, and her room is like a rubbish tip. What can I do?

Open up a dialogue with your daughter about what is and is not acceptable. Encourage her to take responsibility for her space. Point out the key areas of your concern, and be generous over the things that are important to her. Agree on areas that can be messy for short periods, and help her to clear clutter from the rest.

I live in a busy household with my partner, three children, and four cats and dogs. We never seem to get time to rest and our home is always a mess.

Set up your space so that the key family functions are covered. Call in expert help to get bedroom placement right for each child. Make sure your bedroom takes absolute priority in terms of position and decor, and get the whole family involved in clearing the clutter.

My son cannot concentrate on his schoolwork for longer than a few minutes. I often catch him staring out of the window in his room instead of doing his homework. What can I do to help him?

Move his desk away from the window to a place where he can concentrate easily. Check that he is not being disturbed from behind and that he does not have his back to a door. Ask him if there are changes he would like to make.

My wife likes country-style decor with pine furniture and baskets of flowers, whereas I would like something more adventurous and modern. What would you suggest?

Compromise: allow your wife to have baskets of flowers (which cheer up a space without creating abrasive energy), and get her to agree to a rethink about the furniture.

My girlfriend and I have just moved into a new flat, but we keep getting unexpected visits from friends and neighbours. What could be the problem?

Check the front door. If it is red, consider changing the colour to blue. If it is south-facing, put a couple of pots of flowers in front of the door, if possible, to protect it. Shiny door furniture will help to reflect the energy away.

An elderly relative is coming to live with us. What can I do with the Feng Shui of the house to make him happy?

Ask him how he would like things to be arranged. He may want to feel very much involved in the family, or he may prefer a little privacy. If there is a wide choice of rooms, go for an east-facing bedroom, but avoid placing his room between you and your children.

Our teenage son still lives with us, but he is hardly ever in. What can I do to make him feel more involved with the family?

Is your house appropriately set up to include him? Is there space in the sitting room for him to entertain his friends? Is he allowed to use the kitchen to cook and eat in? Also arrange his bedroom so that it is large and private enough for him to feel comfortable there.

We are going to have a live-in nanny. How should we arrange her room?

Your nanny's room should be accessible to the children, but not between your room and theirs. Make sure it has a good view, with uplifting, spring-like colours such as yellow, pale green, peach or dusky pink. Avoid blue and lilac, which may make her feel isolated. Also avoid red, dark brown or black.

I enjoy living on my own, but I miss my friends – they are all in relationships now. Is it possible to rearrange my home to help my social life?

Yes, make the approach to your home more welcoming. Clear and sweep your path, oil the hinges of your gate, hang a picture of a happy group of people in your hall and arrange your furniture for social situations.

I am living with people who argue all the time. How can I make the atmosphere more harmonious?

The easiest way to transform your space when you come home is to play some beautiful music and open the windows to release some of the grief and get the positive energy flowing. When you have time, try to rearrange the furniture for support rather than confrontation, for example, chairs at right angles instead of facing each other.

8

feng shui in the garden

庭園之風水

The land around your house should have special meaning for you and the other occupants of your household. Once you have crossed over the boundary, your spirits should lift and your heart soften. What better greeting could you have when you return, than seeing a lovingly cared for outside space? As each plant or tree blossoms and thrives, it is a celebration of life itself.

The approach to your home, and the garden surrounding it, sets the tone for the quality of chi inside the building and how it will affect the occupants. Always look at the proportion of land in relation to the building, and the way the house sits on the land. The plot needs to be balanced in size and shape against your home and any outbuildings. The balance of land to either side is also important, and so is the gradient of the land.

A large house on a small plot will always make the occupants feel restricted and limited. A house with lots of garden at the front and side, and none to the back, will be struggling for support because of its inadequate tortoise energy. No front garden at all, and a closed aspect in front of a house, deprives it of its phoenix energy. The residents of such a property may suffer from a lack of energy and inspiration, and feel stifled.

Begin by assessing your garden in terms of tortoise, dragon, tiger and phoenix energy (see pages 34–39). Look at the overall quality of the land and air, and the ways they combine to allow plants and trees to grow. Keep the energy clean by practising organic gardening and freeing the land from all chemical contamination.

Remedy a lack of phoenix energy by adding plants and flowers, wherever you can, by the front door. If you lack space, a window box or hanging basket can become your garden, planted to attract butterflies and birds. Using containers to reflect the best of every season will attract vibrant energy to your home. Bright, open, vigorous planting

FAR LEFT **When the tiger, phoenix, dragon and tortoise energies are balanced around your home, you will find that your spirits lift and your heart relaxes in the knowledge that you are well supported, with a clear outlook ahead of you.**

ABOVE **A window box or hanging basket with bright flowers at the front of your home will attract vibrant phoenix** energy and all the opportunities and useful contacts that it brings with it. This will help you to improve your future prospects.

BELOW **If your back garden is too small to accommodate a tree, bamboo is a good alternative for supplying your home with supporting tortoise chi.**

at the front of your house will help you to remain open to future experiences, while considered design at the rear will help nourish and repair any weakness in your past, especially childhood influences.

Opt for strong planting and uplifting design in the back garden. Acknowledge the excellent job a grand old tree is doing, and add some sculpture or a statue to support it in its work of creating stability and form. A sturdy garden wall at the back of the house will also help to increase the amount of tortoise energy available.

A garden sloping away at the back allows chi to run away, so needs help to lift the chi back up. Add structures or plants to achieve this: trees in a large garden, plants, for example bamboo, in a smaller garden, also trellises and well-designed brick walls or fences.

Any land to the sides of the building needs to balance and gently hold the energy of the building without squeezing it in. Remove any plants, shrubs or trees that loom over the building or choke it. Be wary of too many creeping, climbing plants, especially when they begin to encroach on windows or doors.

Proportion and perspective are very important when designing your garden. Consider your space as a link between outside and inside, which allows the energy of the landscape to soften and mellow as it approaches the house. Work always with the idea of that movement between the outside and the inside, seeing the moment of change as a pause in the breath of chi as it travels into your home. You can obscure the boundary between the interior and the exterior of your home by opening windows and doors. The building could even be seen as a gently tamed and sheltered outdoor space but, as a sudden storm will remind you, the garden can never really be thought of as an outside room.

FAR LEFT **Consider the movement of energy between the outside of your home and the inside, and how your garden can be designed to blur the boundary between the two.**

97

LEFT **T**his is a good
example of a water-
dominated garden,
with its curved stone
seat set in a recess,
echoing a gentle
meandering energy
that is conducive to
meditation and
contemplation in
peaceful surroundings.

RIGHT **W**ater chi
gives a garden
gentleness, stillness
and peace, and
creates a space for
contemplation but
without any feeling
of depression or
dreariness.

WATER ENERGY: THE CONTEMPLATIVE GARDEN

It is a good idea to design your garden, or areas of your garden, according to the five elements. *(see page 21).* An entire garden, or area of land, can lean more towards the expression of one particular element than another. This is its keynote, or main theme, but does not suggest that it is the only quality present.

Spend some time in your garden, and you will soon come to know its energetic qualities and how best to allow them expression. It is an inspiring way of letting a space develop and emerge in its true colours. Supporting the natural chi of an area creates a space that will not need hours of constant toil, and every connection to it will be mutually nourishing and inspiring.

In a contemplative, water energy garden, the space feels still and quiet, without being depressing or dreary. Its natural contours are gently undulating and it is a place where wildlife may pause and insects hover. There may be a slight dip or hollowing in the land. You may have already identified this garden as a good place to sit and think, or daydream, or lie on the ground to read a book or write. A curving stone seat in a recess or arbour would be an ideal piece of furniture, but make sure it catches occasional sunlight and warmth.

To enhance the water energy, you could arrange the planting and design to echo curving, fluid shapes and styles. This is a place for a low, tumbling rockery, dense, ground-hugging alpine plants, and scattered flowers winding their way around sun-dappled rocks. A tiny stream tumbling from one pool to another will add life and

ABOVE **E**nclosed
outdoor spaces that
lend themselves to
solitary activities
like thinking, reading
or writing are
considered to be
dominated by the
water element in
Feng Shui. The land in
such a space may
hollow or dip slightly,
and contain blue or
lilac flowers.

BELOW **A** water
energy garden is a
good place for
attracting wildlife,
where birds perch
upon shrubs and
gardening equipment,
and insects hover
in circles.

sparkle, attracting visitors to this calm and tranquil spot. Water is not essential, however, and should be fairly low-key if it forms part of this space.

Soften sharp edges with climbing, rambling plants and allow a certain undisciplined flow to emerge. This is not a place for rigid pruning and sharp style, rather a place of flow and rhythm.

Planting needs to reflect this flow, with colours blending and toning, and scatterings of flowers and foliage rather than large clumps or rigid lines. Tones of blue and lilac would work well here. Self-seeded plants will add an air of the unexpected, preventing any stagnation or repression of the easy flow of energy.

A water-dominated area of a garden may be a good starting point for work on the rest of the plot. One sunlit winter morning, wrap yourself up well and go out there with a hot drink and a rug, and dream the rest of the garden into being. You may suddenly find yourself joined by birds and other wildlife that like being where the action is.

ABOVE **Circular ponds and curving paths winding through low-lying clumps of foliage and rambling plants are perfect for a contemplative garden.** **The colours of scattered flowers and foliage should blend naturally into the scene without disturbing the tranquillity.**

RIGHT **In Feng Shui, wood chi symbolizes the rising energies of new growth. A wood energy area is often a place where the land rises or tall plants and trees grow upwards very quickly.**

RIGHT **Cutting hedges into strong, straight lines will add wood energy to a garden, and so will repairing broken fences, walls and other architectural features.**

RIGHT **The metal energy of this highly shaped plant will keep an excess of wood energy in check.**

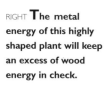

WOOD ENERGY: THE GARDENER'S GARDEN

With the first surge in growth that signals the coming of spring, the wood energy garden comes to life. This is the place where the powerful impetus of wood's rising energy makes itself felt, as apparently dead branches stir into life, and the first buds unfurl. A rising gradient of land, and trees or lofty plants thrusting upwards towards the sky, may identify a wood energy location for you, and will tell you that this is a place for new growth and movement. It is ideal for your greenhouse or tool shed (not a junk-filled shed). You could also put your cold frames here, some starter beds and places for growing small plants and seedlings.

The wood energy garden is the place for new beginnings, revitalized energy, and action. If your garden feels stale and tired, cultivate wood energy by introducing tall plants and seeing that new growth is encouraged. Careful pruning of existing trees and shrubs admits light and provides space for transformation.

ABOVE **Cut back and carefully prune shrubs to encourage wood energy to increase in your garden. Most noticeable in spring, this chi makes its power felt in new shoots pushing up through barren soil.**

In the early spring, take a good look at your garden and decide on a thorough clearing of clutter. You will need to walk all the way round and list all the things that need sorting out, mending or removing. Make a note to remove obvious items such as broken pots, canes and garden paraphernalia, but also consider thinning out plants, and pruning trees and shrubs.

Repeat this process at any time of year when plants seem to be struggling, repairing broken architectural features, walls or fencing. You will be amazed at the effect such a garden pick-me-up will have on the vitality of your plants.

Every garden needs planning and organizational work. Make sure you are ready to put those plans into motion with appropriate equipment and tools. Keep everything tidy, clean and well maintained, and encourage anybody else who works in the garden to do the same. There is nothing more frustrating than having an idea for some work in the garden only to be thwarted because you cannot find the appropriate tool, or someone has used up the last of something and not replaced it.

Feng Shui suggests that in order to allow your garden to change and develop, strong, straight lines should be introduced to architectural details and planting. Topiary will redefine those unruly hedges, and straight paths will give purpose to a sloping lawn. A straight path flanked by trees, or a row of tall flowers at a border's edge, can transform a depressed or stagnating garden.

Subtler remedies include giving lawns or flower-beds sharper edges, or adding structure to the garden by way of plots specifically set aside for different plantings. A well-stocked vegetable garden with rows and squares of plants will increase wood energy, bringing with it the need for meticulous planning, careful organization, and a resulting avalanche of new and changing growth.

I once saw a walled garden where the energy of what was a slightly tired space had been uplifted by the addition of a gate. It worked by instilling the idea that there was somewhere to expand into or to move towards. Introducing the appearance, if not the reality, of something beyond the eye will always benefit your garden.

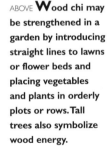

ABOVE **W**ood chi may be strengthened in a garden by introducing straight lines to lawns or flower beds and placing vegetables and plants in orderly plots or rows. Tall trees also symbolize wood energy.

RIGHT **A** garden gate, or a door set in a garden wall leading to another, unseen place, is also a form of wood energy. The gate can provide the illusion of an extension to your garden, and the unseen place beyond will increase curiosity to see it, and uplift the spirits.

RIGHT **According to Feng Shui, the moment in summer when trees and plants are flowering most gloriously represents the expansive nature of fire energy.**

FIRE ENERGY: ENTERTAINMENT AND ACTION

High summer sees the flourishing of fire energy, when activity and purpose inhabit every garden. This is the time when flowers are at their finest, trees spread high and wide into the sky, and emerald lawns stretch out waiting for people to make use of them. Plant life is in perpetual motion, and the odd moment of quiet is simply preparation for another flurry of flowers.

The garden is set like a stage for action, and has a great capacity for fire energy. But look closer and you will find places for rest, as well as evidence of forethought and planning, structure, design and clarity interwoven amongst the space. Creating a garden that is well-balanced enough to incorporate fire energy into whatever other elemental energy it naturally assumes, is quite an achievement and is well worth the effort.

If you find you have created a wonderful space with strong water energy, where you can sit alone quietly at the end of the day and contemplate future projects, but where you would also like to be able to enjoy other, more lively events at certain times, then you can remedy this by adding fire energy.

FAR RIGHT **Shrubs with pointed leaves and sharp or 'leaping flame' shapes incite action and add fire energy to a garden.**

ABOVE **A tree-house, or anything that brings a sense of fun into your garden, represents fire chi.**

CREATING SPACE FOR RECREATION

The most obvious starting point is to consider the structure of the garden. You may have set aside ample space to grow vegetables, cultivate small plants, create shrub borders and flower-beds, even to establish an orchard, but is there room for entertainment?

A garden with areas for play amongst its lawns and pathways will always stay lively and active. Any amount of other elemental energies, such as blue and white planting, meandering paths and solitary corners, will then be enlivened by people having fun. A croquet lawn, a pathway drawn for hopscotch, stepping stones across a stream, a patio marked as a chessboard with very large game pieces ready for action, are all features that will add sparkle to rigidly structured or tired gardens.

Between the planning stage and the moment of harvest, the garden needs time and space to flower and show off. A plant needs to flower before it will fruit, and a garden needs fire energy to complete its circle of existence.

If children regularly use the garden, their actions will give you all the ideas you need, but stop short of allowing a full-blown game of football. Give your children a swing, a tree-house or a see-saw. Anything that helps them to run, jump and climb will boost the garden's fire energy. Family pets and other animals fulfil the same function.

庭園之風水

REMEDY YOUR LIFE

Many people complain that they never have time to enjoy their homes or gardens. Often the problem arises because there is a lack of fire energy – no places for fun, good humour or light-heartedness. If this is an issue for you, it may be easier to sort out the garden first. Are you inviting in action and passion, or signalling to the universe that, if and when you have got everything right, you might be able to stop for a cup of tea and a look at next year's seed catalogue?

Every person, every home and every garden needs a bit of a spark. Sweeps of ground-hugging shrubs that give way to rambling roses, and paths that curve and flow, have their purposes, but will never stir anybody into action. Next time you are choosing plants, look for some electrifying shapes and colours, rising points and leaping flame shapes. A flash of crimson and orange, or a swathe of scarlet will boost the garden's active potential and make you smile. Create areas that will draw your eye and hold your attention: place a

group of potted geraniums along the top of a wall; in winter fill a well-positioned greenhouse with scarlet flowering plants and paint the door frame to match. Always make sure there is room in your garden for berry-bearing shrubs and trees that will stay alive with the activity of birds foraging for food throughout the coldest months.

Make sure you have a decent spot for entertaining. An elevated area in the garden, or one that makes guests go across or around the garden before they get to it, is more stimulating than a convenient place outside the back door. Put an octagonal table in front of the best view in the garden, and top it off with a parasol and some

candles to light as evening draws on. The spectacle of the host arriving with a tray laden with food and drinks will also add a touch of theatre to al-fresco entertaining, and cooking the food outside will add to fire energy.

LEFT **G**arden lights, candles and flares can illuminate your garden at night in a spectacular way. Coupled with some stimulating company and lively conversation, the lighting will add a blaze of fire energy to your garden.

ABOVE **B**right orange or scarlet flowers, grown in beds or in pots along the top of a wall, will promote fire energy. Berry bushes attract foraging birds, even during winter, and enhance fire chi.

RIGHT **A stable foundation for all gardens, the earth element collects into itself all the splendour of nature during winter, where debris such as dead leaves protects and enriches it for the following spring.**

ABOVE **In order to promote good earth energy, soil needs to be protected. However, a garden needs frost as well as** **sun to give it life. A few small piles of dead wood, flowers gone to seed, and fallen leaves can be left to overwinter there.**

EARTH ENERGY: IN TOUCH WITH NATURE

You can recognize an earth energy garden because it blooms and blossoms, seeds and weathers in a bountiful way throughout the year. It is truly the garden of all seasons, and we can make good use of all the resources this garden provides.

The transforming quality of earth chi enables the great cyclical movements and changes to take place that are part of life. Life in the garden is no exception. When creating a space high in earth energy, it is important to honour, in the garden's design and planting, the full cycle of life and death. In spring the garden will need places for insects and birds to nest, and in autumn enough unsheltered space for the wind to do its work. A few piles of leaves and fallen wood can be left to overwinter in the space, some dead flowers can be left to go to seed, and some moss allowed to gather.

ABOVE **All that happens naturally in a garden during the year has a function. Even fungus should be allowed to grow, because it has a purpose in the creation of the garden's health and good earth chi.**

Good management of the garden, by protecting the soil from damage and erosion, and considerate planting of trees and plants, will greatly help the quality of the earth energy. The fertility of the soil must be protected, of course, but an earth energy garden also needs rain, wind and frost, as well as sun, to give it life. Avoid introducing earth energy-depleting plants and practices. Plants that have been imported from another grower, force-fed, hybridized and installed purely as accessories to our lifestyle and image of ourselves, will not have good earth energy. Neither will space previously used to accommodate caged animals, or to grow plants with the sole purpose of screening out unwanted sights. Such places will need to be left to rest for a while before being used again. Likewise, a garden stripped in the autumn of all unsightly dead matter, and then left bare all winter, will not have beneficial earth energy.

All the resources of the garden, including the unwelcome visitors such as fungi and so-called garden pests including slugs, snails and

庭園之風水

aphids, have a place in this space and, if all these are scoured out of existence, what is left will probably need to be kept alive with the assistance of fertilizers and pesticides.

The sure way to have good earth energy in a garden is to consider the role and purpose of everything that is already there when you take the garden on, before interfering with it. You should also make an effort to create space for things that would occur naturally in the wild, but which the garden lacks. Imagine, for example, the contribution that two tiny ponds could make to the garden, if set up in such a way that they provide a useful watering hole for wildlife. The wild creatures attracted into the garden would help to perform a wide range of duties that would normally have to be managed artificially in their absence, for example, keeping plant-eating pests such as snails and slugs at bay.

RIGHT **An earth garden exudes practicality, resourcefulness and an air of 'work in progress'. You will need a compost heap and space for a fire to burn garden waste.**

A GARDEN FOR ALL SEASONS

Creating a space with balanced earth energy requires recognition of a garden's natural rhythm and pace, and learning to appreciate the usefulness of all things. So we should find ways to celebrate, for example, the excess of mud that early spring brings as much as we welcome the wealth of growth that the mud will encourage. Look at the garden as a resource centre.

For example, if your garden becomes a brittle, disused wasteland in winter, then you should consider letting features develop that will allow it to transform into a crystalline wonderland. Consider the effect of deciduous trees, which take on a new shape and atmosphere when they are stripped of their foliage and the late winter sun filters through their branches. The stark branches are an ever-changing framework – sometimes frosted with white, at other times hung all about with raindrops.

In autumn, petals may fall away, but they yield to tightly bound seeds and kernels, and leaves gather around the garden to muffle sharp edges and slow down the gathering chi.

Perhaps the only earth energy imbalance a lot of gardens ever experience is our inability to fully appreciate the quieter delights of so-called 'unseasonable' times.

Crunching across a frosty lawn to gather mistletoe from an old apple tree or collect swathes of twisted willow to bring indoors will help us to recognize that the garden has something to offer all year round.

Unshowy plants often have much more to offer than it would appear at first glance. Many gardeners I know grow certain plants simply for the way their foliage holds the morning dew. Learn to appreciate plants at all stages of growth and degeneration.

Space for a large fire to burn things, and a well-managed compost heap, will become essential items. You should also have plenty of room to move around the garden, especially to gather and sow.

RIGHT **Metal energy
is associated with
autumn and the time
of harvest. Natural
contours that keep
lines fluid in a sparse
yet complete way
symbolize metal chi.**

METAL ENERGY: STYLED, STRUCTURED SPACE

As the gardening year approaches harvest time, the effects of balanced metal energy consolidate themselves. The rewards of previous labour are reaped, fruits are gathered, and grain stored. Metal energy is at play, transforming the resources of earth to enable them to lie low throughout winter.

A garden that is rich in metal energy is sparse, of unusual design and content, with carefully placed features. The motivating spirit behind it is clarity and conciseness, and the design is strong because of its purposefulness and because it does useful work in continuing the life of the garden. To fulfil this function and increase the metal energy into your garden, try adding features such as a strategically placed old bench, a piece of sculpture from stone or marble, or a carefully sited semicircle of trees.

When working with metal energy outside in this way, look at the form that lies beneath the growth of plants, trees and grass. Think about accentuating the garden's natural contours with design that adds to its innate structure, and keep lines fluid. Remember also that less is more. The quality of each item should be carefully considered before being allowed a place in the garden.

LEFT **Plants with white
or silver flowers and
foliage, planted in
circles within a larger
garden, will introduce
metal energy.**

REFINEMENT AND COMPLETION

Introducing metal energy into the garden will involve refining and reducing it to its essential nature, and creating features around this theme. A circle is a good shape to use when working with metal energy, with colour and shape designed to spiral, or turn upon, an energetic fulcrum or pivot.

To add the transforming quality of metal to the whole garden, try to include circular gardens within the main garden. They could perhaps be scented, with white and silver as the main colours. Include white flowering shrubs, plants with silver foliage, or foliage with round leaves.

Completion is a guiding theme here, with tasks designed to move things towards their conclusion. To this end, fences and walls should be repaired, and loose ends tied up.

WHAT OUR GARDENS TELL US ABOUT OURSELVES

Looking at the garden in terms of energy brings a whole new dimension to the way we create our outdoor space, or the way – we now notice – that it creates us. A garden displaying signs of imbalance in one element can be remedied; specific activities, such as contemplation or entertainment, can be consciously fostered.

In addition to looking at the way our home rests on its plot, taking into consideration phoenix, dragon, tiger, snake and tortoise energy, as well as considering the broader landscape beyond our home and how it is related to our own energy, we can now add an assessment of the elemental make-up of our gardens to help us understand the way our life is unfolding, and then make decisions about the areas that need greater support. For example, people who find it difficult to complete tasks can work to boost the metal energy in their gardens. As we have seen, the five elements and their productive and shaping cycles *(see page 21)* can also be used to correct imbalances and support the garden. As with the interior of your home, you will need to ask yourself why you have chosen this outdoor space, and what it tells you about yourself.

The enlightenment to be gained from working in the garden in this way may therefore be very revealing. We may be well practised at creating careful interiors, but it is more challenging, and rewarding, to cultivate and understand the outdoors.

BELOW **Strategically placed pathways, outdoor furniture, hedges and trees spiralling from or turning around a central point, indicate a garden where metal energy predominates.**

Furniture in metal and stone

Clipped, rounded items

Spiral sculpture symbolizes metal

Silver foliage

Curved hedges

Sparse yet complete planting

8

feng shui in the garden

TOP 10 QUESTIONS

庭園之風水

I have a line of trees in my front garden. Should I cut them down?
What would be heading towards the house if the trees were not there? If they are shielding you from a T-junction or electricity pylon, think again. Not all trees at the front of a house have a negative effect, but if you are thinking of removing them, you are probably ready to meet whatever will come your way once the trees are removed.

I have a recurrent problem with weeds in my garden. How can I keep the weeds at bay?
Gardeners will say you need to improve the quality of your soil – this means the quality of your life in Feng Shui terms. The weeds may be representing what you are attracting into your life. Learn how to stop the weeds in the first place, rather than making it a life's work trying to remove them later.

I have a lot of ivy in my garden. Will this block the chi?
Ivy growing out of control can represent clinging, stagnant chi, especially if mature trees have also become covered. Gradually prune or remove the ivy at the periphery first, then work towards any trees and the house. Ivy obscures things, and you may find that causes of problems surface when you begin to remove it, so do it gradually.

Would adding a conservatory to our garden be a good idea?
Check to see which direction your conservatory would face, then check the elements chart on page 21. A conservatory represents fire, especially one with a pointed roof, so avoid positioning it to face south because you will be fuelling fire: you may become famous or infamous, or find the pace of your life becomes too fast.

I have a patch of weeds in my garden that look very pretty. I am tempted to keep them, but will they affect the chi in a negative way?

Absolutely not. If you like them, keep them. Weeds are a part of life and have a valuable part to play. Just do not let them grow out of control in your garden.

Our garden is always full of cats, and wasps in the summer. Why?

Cats and wasps are attracted to negative energy. Look for trees that are crooked or covered with ivy. Check walls for cracks or loose pointing. Check the grass for moss patches. If you find any of these defects, call a Feng Shui consultant. Otherwise you can deal with it yourself by removing clutter and space clearing.

My parents have offered us some of their garden furniture, but they have had some major problems recently. Should we accept it?

Follow your instincts. If you are worried about the energy, put the furniture in an open, airy position where it will be cleansed by the elements. Do not put it in a cramped spot near your home.

How can I create a really healthy garden using Feng Shui?

The key to a healthy garden is balance. Aim to give expression to all five elements within the space of your garden, and remember to include variety in your planting and architectural detail. Try to grow from seed, or use cuttings from friends' and neighbours' gardens in order to make your success rate higher.

My wife likes the idea of a cottage garden, with a mass of rambling flowers and herbs. I would like something more formal. What would you suggest?

You could have a good structure, with some rambling plants within that order. The combination of expansion and structure is very powerful and beneficial (a mixture of Yin and Yang).

My cat goes to the toilet at the back of the garden. Is this having a bad effect on the energy there?

Watch with interest where your cat is choosing to go to the toilet. Cats are attracted to areas in need of attention. It will only become a matter of concern, however, when cats from neighbouring houses start coming in. If this is the case, a space clear will be necessary.

9

dealing with major changes in life

面对生命中 之主要转变

The nature of life is change. This is not a new idea, but dealing with the reality of change is something many of us find difficult. A lot of us spend much of our time in a 'semi-conscious' state, going through the motions of being alive, and only occasionally experiencing a moment of full awareness before retreating back into habitual patterns and reference points. It is only when life thrusts a dramatic change on us that we are forced to pay attention in a 'moment to moment' way.

The way we drift along on autopilot, barely recognizing how we use our time and space, does not help us to improve our lives. We need to become fully aware and alive to every opportunity in order to develop strategies that will help us move on, grow and develop. But letting go of the past is not always comfortable, or easy. Recollections of past occasions, perhaps with attendant memories of failure and inadequacy, may loom uncomfortably close. You may even fear that current events are echoing these experiences.

Meanwhile, the pursuit of success is often taken for granted. It is what is expected, even demanded of us. Very often, at the forefront of our consciousness, the pressure to succeed nags away. We pile up the pressure on ourselves, and measure our success rate in an alarming array of ways, such as performance tests to pass or fail, so that we can move on to harder and more complicated evaluations of self-worth.

Ingrained habits and the pressure to succeed take their toll: we may get so weighed down by these that we are unable to stand back and gain a realistic perspective on our current circumstances. It is only when we try to change, or when we attempt to navigate a new step in our life's journey, that we boost our level of insight and live fully in the present. At these times of increased self-awareness, it is often the case that other people latch on to this and begin to watch us with interest, perhaps deriving inspiration from our journey.

FAR LEFT **Important changes in your life can stir you into full waking consciousness and force you to confront issues that normally lie dormant while you go about your everyday tasks.**

面对生命中之主要转变

USING FENG SHUI TO COPE WITH CHANGE

So what can we do to make change truly exciting and empowering, to let go of the stress and let in the good times? The obvious answer is to transform the Feng Shui of our living space so that it supports the process from start to finish, and allows everything to flow as smoothly as possible.

We need to view any opportunity for radical change as a doorway opening in our lives, inviting us to walk through. Look around your space and consider which features of it you would like to take with you, and which ones should be left behind. If you try to squeeze through that doorway with all your old possessions, as though nothing has changed, old problems will resurface and create difficulties and stress. So, at the same time as recreating ourselves, we need to refashion our space.

This chapter will be focusing on the upheavals of moving home and changing partners, but Feng Shui can help you with a wide variety of important turning points in your life, including negotiating a career shift, starting or completing a course of study, altering the direction of your life, health problems, or any other changes you may experience or wish to bring into your life.

The Feng Shui techniques in this chapter include rituals to help you tackle various stages in your life, and practical ways to help you cope with the emotional turbulence that changes can precipitate. Once you have become adept at understanding the ways you can support yourself and have started to practise them, you will find that you can happily let go of the past and move forward to take on new opportunities.

ABOVE **Feng Shui can help newlyweds create a home that will cement and support their relationship and help them to adjust to living together.**

BELOW **Feng Shui will prove invaluable to people undergoing major changes in life, such as finishing a degree course, selling a home, starting a new career, or adjusting to a change in physical health.**

WHEN A PARTNER MOVES OUT

I am often called in to help people rebuild their lives after partners have moved out. Very often a person will have been making concerted efforts to make a new life without his or her partner. Whether or not the final decision to split was mutual or one-sided, reached after a long struggle to sort things out and make them work, my client will be experiencing an array of emotions that can be very stressful, if not debilitating.

GETTING HELP

Calling in someone to help often marks a moment of change, so this is a time when I would always recommend that you work on the Feng Shui of your space with someone else. If no one is available, try looking at the earth energy of your space for clues as to how to proceed. Remove your partner's remaining possessions straight away, or at least put them near an exit point in your space to signal that they are on their way out.

ABOVE **It may be particularly difficult to get rid of jewellery or other objects closely associated with an ex-partner. You should do so, however, to make way for new times.**

MOVING OUT THE MEMORIES

You may need to revisit memories before you can let them go. For example, before you can throw out an item purchased during your time together, you have to recall the time your partner bought the object, brought it home and showed it to you. This process can stir many emotions and should be undertaken with care. The item you are considering may have been an emotional landmark in your relationship, and in order to let go of it you must discard the expectations that surrounded it. What seems to be merely a set of towels may have represented what you thought was the beginning of a life together, and shared expectations, taste and ideals. No wonder it is difficult to throw them away.

On many occasions I have sat on the edge of a client's bed, listening to how that person has done everything possible to let go of the past and attract someone new, only to find that the bed I am sitting on – which that person sleeps in every night – is the very bed my client shared with his or her partner.

Likewise, a glance at your hand will tell you if your jewellery needs to move on too. Precious metals and gemstones carry a powerful energetic punch, an encoded history of exchange and patterning. With that in mind, you should consider the effect your jewellery is having on your life, and replace any items that are holding you back.

BELOW **What may simply be a set of towels to someone else may have a special significance for you. You may need to recall the memories some items evoke before you can part with them.**

ADJUSTING TO BEING SINGLE

While you are moving out your partner's belongings, you will need to rearrange your space to suit your needs as a single person. Look around your home for design features and items that suited the couple you were once part of, and transform the space into a perfect place for one person. This may mean rearranging a dining room for less formal entertaining perhaps, or turning it into a place where you can pursue your hobbies and interests. Furniture and decor which catered to your needs as a couple may need to be changed.

Colours that foster intimacy and sharing, such as warm pinks and peaches, could be replaced with shades of blue to encourage calm and contemplation, violet to aid spiritual growth and transformation, or green hues to reflect your desire for a new beginning. Splashes of red will support your self-esteem and enable you to get back into society when the time is right. A lovely way to herald that moment is to place a mass of flame-coloured flowers in the bedroom and hallway.

Reassess the contents, colour scheme and layout of every room and give them a new lease of life to signal to the world that you are entering a different phase. In this way, Feng Shui is like a daily affirmation of your new status. To create a feeling of calm and tranquillity, introduce aquamarine, pale blues and more depth and texture into your fabrics. Replace unframed, angular mirrors with smaller, oval-framed ones. Add touches of gold where they will catch the light, and table lamps with soft, pleated or swathed shades. Turn off overhead lights, and create places where you can enjoy your own company without being faced by the reminder of an empty chair or an empty set of pillows.

Make your bathroom into a place of relaxation and delight, with serene blues and greens. In the kitchen, discard cookware that is bigger than you need and treat yourself to place settings perfect for one.

When you are ready to recreate your life, add spring colours to your bedroom. Fresh greens softened with pale yellow will encourage personal growth. Replace carpeting with natural wooden flooring to add glow and sheen to your living space. Exchange heavy drapes for crisper, bolder fabrics and designs. Try leaving a window bare, with just a twist of fabric to soften the edges and catch the light. Increase light levels by moving heavy furniture away from windows, or replacing it with less cumbersome, more frivolous pieces. Decorate a room predominantly in violet – an excellent colour for a time like this – then buy yourself a new broom and sweep a clean pathway to your front door, which you could adorn with some new fittings.

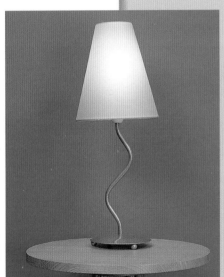

BELOW **It is important to remove from your home things that were suited to the couple you were part of, and to introduce items that now fit your new status as a single person.**

ABOVE **Create a pleasant environment suited to your own tastes and needs, and set up little areas where you can enjoy your own company. Vases of flowers and comfortable places to sit may help.**

面
对
生
命
中

WHEN A NEW PARTNER MOVES IN

I was once called in to help a man and woman whose relationship had steadily been going wrong since they started to live together. He had moved in a few months previously and now they were on the verge of splitting up.

FAR RIGHT **A home undergoes a change of energy when its inhabitants change. The new occupant of your home should be involved in rearranging or even redecorating what will be a home for you both.**

I sat with the woman in the bedroom of her beautiful home pondering possible solutions to her problem, and there both the problem and solution were spread out before us in many different ways. The woman had been so well established as a single person, and so effective was her space, that this new resident could make no impact on it at all. She wanted him in her life, but she had not seen the necessity of changing anything in her home to accommodate him.

With barely enough room to hang his clothes or put his toothbrush, he was occupying the space in the way that a guest who is very aware of being unwelcome perches in a chair nearest to the door to drink the proffered meagre cup of coffee, before swiftly taking leave. The message her living space was inadvertently giving him was "I'm not prepared to open up and really let you in".

BELOW **If you only give space to your partner grudgingly, you will be giving out the wrong message and may be perceived as selfish, thoughtless and even a little mean.**

Excuses such as "he's only just moved in" or "it may not work out" or "I don't want to scare him off" are not good reasons to withhold opening up your space to accommodate two people. In fact, keeping your space just the way it is, only clearing a few drawers and letting your partner fit in around you, is the best way to let her or him think that you do not care.

Shared space, and space to call your own within the whole, are both essential. Your willingness to allow someone into your space may reveal just how ready you are to give of yourself. The areas you are less happy to share will tell you a lot about the level of intimacy you and your partner want.

RIGHT **Living with another person means making sure there is plenty of space and storage to keep personal belongings.**

面對生命中之重要轉變

SHARED SPACE AND PRIVATE SPACE

If your partner is moving in, be prepared to rearrange things or throw them out, and to redesign and redecorate to support your new life together. You can start small and build up, but expect to change. You will need to transform your space to encourage trust and commitment, so get rid of colours such as black, beige and blue and replace them with the warm earth colours often associated with Asia and the Middle East, such as saffron, ochre, amber and terracotta, perhaps brushed with gold. If you feel that these exotic shades will play havoc with your colour scheme, try a more European version using the colours of ripe peaches and pale gold pears, the colours of Tuscany and Florence, or of late summer sun. You could start by painting the kitchen yellow, or changing all your blue bedlinen for peach (or orange if you are ready to let things happen more quickly).

In order to relax and enjoy each other's company to the full, you should ensure that the furniture and its placement accommodates two people comfortably. Position two chairs to catch the best view, make room for two people to use the office comfortably, and arrange the kitchen so that cooking together is a real pleasure rather than an edgy battle for space. Use the home to give you insight into what is happening between you. Utilize the way you negotiate your space to feed back into your understanding of the relationship, and the ways in which you can help to make it work.

If your partner cannot even find the space to hang a coat, let alone put a toothbrush in the bathroom or store CDs in your cabinet, you may have some serious work to do. However, if all is well until it comes to sharing office space, then you might consider separate territory for this part of your life.

Brighten up the area immediately outside your front door and clear the hallway of anything that clutters or crowds it. Look at the space at the centre of the household and be ruthless about clearing it. Allow only objects of great simplicity and beauty to occupy it.

Ensure that the boundaries of your property are suitable and are doing their job properly, and then go indoors and clear any passageways. Mend broken door handles and free any doors that jam or stick. Check that windows are clean and uncluttered, and pay attention to the quality of flooring throughout the house. You are aiming to attract good quality chi and to keep it flowing easily around your home. You will be continuing to enjoy your sense of self, yet opening up to share with another person. In Feng Shui terms these issues are associated with wood and earth energy, but you should also keep your home well balanced to include fire energy to help your passage from being single to living in a happy and positive way with a partner.

RIGHT **The home must be cleared of items bought for a single person. Replace colours such as** cool blue, black and beige with amber, gold and peach in order to encourage harmony, warmth and trust.

SELLING YOUR HOME

In order to be able to sell your home you must really want to move, and to have accepted that the episode of your life spent there is over. Selling it under any other circumstances is, in my experience, a difficult and potentially hazardous event.

Selling a home is the same as taking any other step forward. In order to accomplish it successfully, you need a clear idea of where you intend to go next, not in terms of the actual place, but in terms of the direction, or new 'life space' that you want to be occupying. If you know that, it will set up the necessary dynamic for you to step out of your old space and sell it.

So if you have decided it is time for you to move, start focusing on the precise features of your current situation that you have outgrown. For the exercise below, you will need two large, clean sheets of paper and some water-soluble coloured pens.

LETTING GO

Take a sheet of paper and a coloured pen, and draw a floor plan of your home. Add as much colour and detail, or as little, as you wish. Then start adding descriptions and labels to list the things about your home that do and do not work for you. Include a reference to the garden and its location. Take your time, and be as free with your comments as you feel you want to be.

When you have finished, pick up a different coloured pen and circle all those comments and features you want to leave behind. Then write at the bottom of the page clearly and boldly, using the same pen, the words 'Thank you and goodbye'.

You could also ritually say farewell to the things that you want to release about your life and home, by putting the 'old page' in a glass bowl of water and leaving it for the writing to disperse and disappear. This is a very effective way of representing the transition from an old way of life to a new one.

MOVING HOUSE CHECKLIST

■ Decide on the new direction you want your life to take.

■ Draw a floor plan of your present home, and list all the features that do and do not work for you.

■ Identify the qualities of your present home that you would like to take to your new home, then copy them on to a fresh piece of paper. Write a 'welcome' greeting at the top of the new page.

■ If necessary, move around each room of your existing home and say goodbye, in order to sever any lingering feelings you may have about wanting to remain in the property.

FAR RIGHT **W**here you live is a reflection of who you are, so if you want to change your home you must broaden your horizons in order to attract the things you are seeking.

FAR LEFT **U**se coloured pens to draw a floor plan of your home, then add descriptions and labels about the things that work and do not work for you.

Selling a house you have loved and lived in for years, where you have spent happy times, and which has seen you through some significant events in your life, can be a difficult thing to manage, even when you know it really is the right thing to do. It may help you to tell yourself that, by hanging on to something no longer truly appropriate for you, you will actually be blocking someone else's ability to move on in their life.

Even if you have not been happy in a house, or you have been unable to achieve what you wanted there, it can still be hard to leave. People sometimes feel that 'unfinished business' is preventing them from selling a home. A couple I once worked with had to spend time moving from room to room saying goodbye and talking about all the things they had and (maybe more significantly) had not done there, before they finally got a buyer for their house (which everyone had expected would sell with tremendous ease).

WELCOMING NEW FEATURES

Take another piece of paper and copy on to it, at random, any part of the drawing or description of your old home that worked particularly well for you and that you would like to enjoy in your new home. Try to use the whole scope of the page, not filling it, but using areas all over it. Then take a different coloured pen and add drawings or words about any new features or qualities you would like to enjoy in your new space. Write at the top of the new page, still using the same pen, the words 'Hello and welcome'.

This is a deceptively simple but excellent way of focusing your intention to sell your current home and move on. Once you have completed the 'new page', pin it up in a prominent position so that you can continue to reflect on it and carry on making refinements; it will also reaffirm your intention every time you pass by and look at it. Put it on a mirror in a place where you often stand, and you will empower it even more.

A REFLECTION OF OURSELVES

If you can sell your home easily, but cannot find anywhere to go, you need to be focusing on allowing radical change in other areas of your life. A space is a reflection of ourselves, and what we attract to us is a reflection of who we are. We cannot expect beauty, light and grace if all we do is watch television and grumble. We need to broaden our horizons and be prepared to let change enter our lives.

FAR RIGHT **You may wish to perform a short ritual to say goodbye to all the things about your life and home that you want to leave behind. You can do this by dissolving the words on your 'old' floor plan in a glass bowl of water.**

TAKING PRACTICAL ACTION

Once we have reached the stage when we have come to a decision about our life and definitely want to sell our home, most of us hope that the sale will happen quickly and easily. There is no reason to delay, and it is time to take practical action to accomplish this.

The first stumbling block to overcome at this point is our possible reluctance to spend any time or effort on the house, now that we have decided to sell it. This is the biggest mistake a home-owner can make. If you can discard this attitude and accept that all investment by you at this time is going to earn a very high return, you will be halfway to success.

Few people want to buy, or to be involved with, an unloved space. They may not explain it in those terms, but this will be the basis of their reasons for not wanting to buy.

People respond to houses on an emotional level. Logic is overruled, and the initial feeling they experience at the front door, or by a window in the hall, is what counts at the end of the day. In order to sell your home, you could do no better than to give it one last round of gifts, one final parting celebration of just how wonderful it is and is going to be for the new owners.

Prepare your home as if you are going to have a major family event or party. This is to be your home's moment of glory, and it should be dressed for the occasion. Give maximum attention to three key areas: the approach to your home, the hall and the kitchen.

BELOW **The view of your house from the street is important and its appearance will affect the quality of chi attracted to it. Ensure it looks its best if you want to sell it.**

THE APPROACH TO YOUR HOME

Look at the front of the building, the main door, and any gateway, garden or drive. The view that a potential buyer has from the street is important. Check the state of windows and the sides of the property.

The message your home needs to give out is 'much loved, abundant and full of opportunity'. A freshly painted door and a porch that has been cleaned and brightened up will attract good chi.

Cut back any climbing, thorny or prickly plants that encroach on the porch or front path. Weed the front garden, refresh any wilted plants and repair paths and fencing.

A well-placed birdbath or feeder will attract and energize positive chi. A small fountain or other moving water feature, sympathetic to the overall design of the property, would also help a sale.

Standing looking at the front door, a glance directly behind you will tell you if any sharp angles directed at your back suggest that something shiny and reflective in the way of door furniture is needed.

RIGHT **The front hall of your house should be inviting and uncluttered. Improve a cramped or narrow** area with a well-placed, framed oval or octagonal mirror, or pictures of sunny landscapes.

THE HALL

Remedy a cramped hall with a framed oval or octagonal mirror. Pictures of widening horizons and sunny landscapes will help, or pictures that show a group of people enjoying themselves. Glass fronts to pictures will lift the flow of chi. In a narrow hall, hang pictures a little higher than usual, and choose an uneven number to prevent stagnation of energy. If stairs can be seen from the front door, or are opposite it, make sure they are well carpeted. If your home suffers from long, straight corridors, a thick rug with a patterned border will calm the energy in the hall. Avoid the colour blue – it will not make visitors feel welcome. Add a glass vase of inspiring flowers. Most people have a good idea of whether or not they want to buy a home before they get any further than the hall, so make an effort there.

THE KITCHEN

The kitchen should be a positive powerhouse, maintaining the chi of the household. Keep the cooker impeccably clean and shining, and make sure you are in the process of cooking (something that everyone likes the smell of) when prospective viewers arrive. Cakes or biscuits are a good choice. The kitchen provides the source of nourishment for the household in terms of food, drink and other things necessary to health and wellbeing, so it needs to reverberate

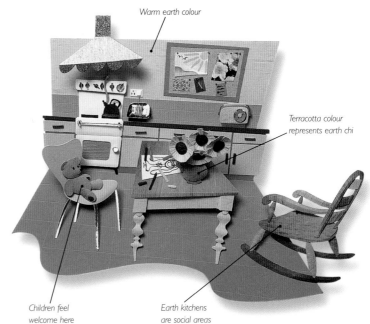

Warm earth colour

Terracotta colour represents earth chi

Children feel welcome here

Earth kitchens are social areas

ABOVE **Your kitchen maintains the chi of your home and it should reverberate with good earth energy. Clean cupboards, windows, floors, curtains and appliances. Bright yellow and cream colours and tempting aromas encourage a cheery atmosphere and should help you to sell your home.**

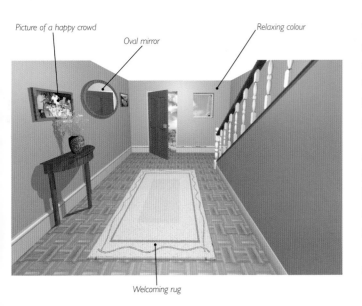

Picture of a happy crowd

Oval mirror

Relaxing colour

Welcoming rug

with good earth energy. It should radiate a message of abundance and good living. Make sure you start by spring-cleaning and clearing clutter, especially in food larders. Clean windows, wash curtains, remove ailing plants, reach to the top of cupboards and behind appliances. Remove anything that does not offer a bright, cheerful, prosperous message, and substitute things that do.

You may need to redecorate, and to renew items. Do not be mean at this moment: like attracts like, and generosity of spirit will be rewarded on all levels. Try using warm, bright yellows and creams in your colour scheme, and square shapes. I would also recommend a red checked tablecloth, a terracotta bowl full of fragrant fruit, or a crystal hung in the window to enhance the chi pouring in.

To prepare a house for sale and attract buyers, a thorough clutter clear, followed by a generic space clear, is essential.

9

dealing with major changes in life

TOP 10 QUESTIONS

面对生命中之主要转变

A house in our street is forever up for sale and changing hands. Is something wrong with it?

Perhaps, but it could just mean that this is a space that will allow people to change and grow quickly. Likewise, a house that has stayed with a family for a long time could mean that the occupants are enjoying a period of contentment, or that the quality of chi there is not allowing them to move on.

We have just bought a terraced house in a narrow street. We do not have a front garden. How can we improve the chi there?

Put hanging baskets of flowers outside the front door, and window boxes wherever possible (not just the ground floor). Add red-berried plants to attract birds and insects. Get the best front door you can afford, and keep it clean and well-painted.

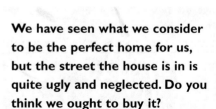

We want to sell our house, which has lots of ivy creeping over the front of it. The ivy gives the house lots of character, but would you advise us to remove it?

If you really like the ivy, then just trim it away from the windows, front porch, door and surround. Make sure that it is not overrunning the house, and keep any gutters clear.

We have seen what we consider to be the perfect home for us, but the street the house is in is quite ugly and neglected. Do you think we ought to buy it?

I would urge you to think very carefully before taking on the energy of this neighbourhood. It would put a drain on your energy levels, and expose you to unwelcome chi from outside. You may end up feeling out of place there.

面对生命中之主要转变

My partner has just moved into my flat. Can I keep a space for myself, or should I share it all?
This is a matter for individual choice, but be aware of which area of your home – and your life – you are keeping from her. It would be better to share everywhere, but introduce opportunities for private space, such as your own desks in a workspace, or your own sinks in the bathroom.

I have recently been made redundant. How can I arrange the Feng Shui of my home to help improve my career prospects?
Your redundancy could be signalling time for a new beginning. Now is the time for inspiration, so have a good clear-out and set some projects in motion, perhaps something creative like painting pictures, sculpture, or arts and crafts.

I have just retired. How should I best arrange my home to help ensure a happy retirement?
Pay particular attention to the west side of your home. Spend more time there, and redecorate or refurbish west-facing rooms with warm, relaxing colours such as peach, apricot, or combinations of pink and green. This will help to support your creativity, while allowing you to free yourself from a more hectic pace of life.

I feel I am ready to begin a new relationship with someone. I have redecorated my flat with warm colours but I am still single.
Perhaps you need to spend time alone to learn more about yourself. You need to move through the whole cycle from the water stage (going within) through to wood (making plans), fire (having fun) before the earth stage will happen.

I have just joined an evening class to study mathematics. How can I arrange my home to help my studies and improve my chances of passing my exams?
Create a good workspace for yourself. Choose a prime position and add the best desk and chair you can afford. Arrange the space for order and make it more Yang to help you get started and to improve your concentration.

I have just had an operation, and want to speed my recovery and get back to optimum health. What would you suggest?
You need an atmosphere of peace and harmony. Sit somewhere light and airy. The place should be spacious, but with a cosy spot to make you feel secure. A place near a window with a good view will help to keep you feeling positive.

121

10

choosing

a new

home

When the time comes for you to choose a new home, a knowledge of Feng Shui astrology, which is based on the classic Chinese book, the *I Ching*, can be extremely useful. Feng Shui astrology *(see page 134)* will help you to determine, at any given time, whether or not it is a good time for you to move, and in which direction it would be best for you to make that move. Having confirmed that your timing and choice of direction are auspicious, Feng Shui principles will help you to make an enlightened decision about the precise location of your new home, the nature of any surrounding land, and the way the home presents itself within the context of that land. Furthermore, an evaluation of the style, construction and design of the new living space will reveal whether or not it will prove to be a supportive place for you. With so much to consider, it would be a good time to call in a professional Feng Shui consultant to help you make the right decision, both for yourself and any other people who will be living with you.

An awareness of the energetics of space will enable you to narrow down your choices considerably, and cut out a lot of the work involved in selecting your new house. If you can focus on the key issues involved, and have a clear idea of the space that will suit your unique needs, you will begin to get a picture of which homes are worth considering and what to be looking out for when you view. If you have worked your way through this book and begun to practise many of the ideas introduced in it, you will now be in a better position to evaluate the Feng Shui of each house you see. Once you have narrowed down the selection to a handful of properties, it will be time to seek extra help in order to make that final decision.

The understanding of Feng Shui you have already gained will be invaluable in setting up a dialogue between you and your consultant, especially when you research the main features of the space together. Pick someone you feel comfortable with, and who is able to communicate with you in a way you understand. There is no reason why anything in Feng Shui should appear obscure or mysterious.

FAR LEFT **When you are looking for a new home, seek help from a consultant who makes you feel at ease. You should consider a property's location, style, construction and design, and also whether it is a good time for you to move.**

挑選新居

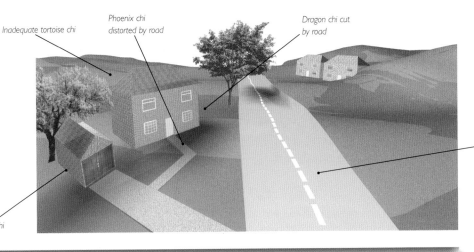

Inadequate tortoise chi

Phoenix chi
distorted by road

Dragon chi cut
by road

Road too near
the house

Tiger chi

RIGHT **If you wish to build your own house, your knowledge of Feng Shui will help you to choose an appropriate landscape for it, and to work with the 'energetics of space' in your new home's design and layout.**

LOOKING AT THE OVERALL PICTURE

If you have decided to build a new home for yourself, your knowledge of Feng Shui will become even more valuable in helping you to oversee the design and layout of the space. If working with the energetics of space has started to become instinctive for you (the likely outcome of having been taught in this way), you will be able to use Feng Shui as an ongoing part of the design process itself, rather than checking designs for good Feng Shui content once they have been drawn up.

If you are using an architect, make sure you use one who is conversant with the basic concepts of Feng Shui and who understands the significance of the structures he or she is designing. Work with the plans as though they are a map, or a picture of your life. Stand well back from the detail and assess the shapes and patterns that will be created when you build your home. Spend a considerable amount of time looking at this bigger picture. It is only time to start considering the precise placement of individual features when the overall theme of the space is thoroughly understood and assessed for its implications on the building's users.

From your study of the five elements or transformations (see page 21), you will be able to work out how shapes, materials and structures affect you, and from your practical application of these ideas you will be able to introduce and balance the particular qualities you find supportive.

It is now time to build on that understanding by exploring the ways in which the energetic impact of the Ba Gua (the eight compass directions — see next page) and the overall shape of a building contribute to the dynamic of a living space. In order to assess the effect a building is having on its occupants, and to remedy it where appropriate, a thorough diagnosis of the space, including its astrology, is vital. Only then can we begin to build on our ability to work with the flow of chi and its impact on our lives. Therefore it is important always to bear in mind that our heightened awareness of the manifestation of chi in the universe is our grounding for all further study and practice. Without it, talking in terms of the way a house or room sits on the land, and how it allows certain qualities to manifest themselves, will not bring any enlightenment to the proceedings, and is a movement away from living our lives as fully empowered human beings.

BELOW **If you decide to move to a city, you should assess how the building you choose will affect its inhabitants. Note how it sits upon the ground and how it is placed in relation to other buildings and land around it.**

MAPPING CHI THROUGH THE BA GUA

The practice of Feng Shui is like a wonderful dance, which is choreographed by the wise and magnificent book the *I Ching*, or *Book of Changes (see page 140)*. This book contains much of the roots of Feng Shui theory and shows us patterns we can use to create our own environment. Its fluent description of the way in which chi manifests itself has become a friend and guide to philosophers and spiritual practitioners everywhere, and no less to women and men who consult it for Feng Shui purposes, and work with the rules for mapping energy that lie within its pages.

The main reference symbol for the practice of Feng Shui is called the Ba Gua, and is derived from the eight trigrams (a diagram made up of three lines, symbolizing the trinity of man, earth and heaven) of the *I Ching*. The Ba Gua is an octagonal figure representing eight paths (plus a ninth, central path) in space and time, and allows us to chart our living space in an unbelievably simple fashion, working at a level of understanding that will suit everyone. The Ba Gua should be laid over a floor plan of your home or your workspace, where it will then reveal which parts of your space relate to particular areas of your life. The result can be both a revelation to the first-time user, and an aid to the experienced practitioner.

ABOVE **This concise version of the Ba Gua shows the eight trigrams and their corresponding elements, colours and compass directions.**

RIGHT **The Ba Gua is an eight-sided diagram representing sacred energy that is described in the *I Ching* (see page 140). It uses time to describe the qualities of a space and how the five transforming elements move within it.**

BELOW **P**lace the Ba Gua over a floor plan of your home to find out how chi is manifesting itself. **This version of the Ba Gua includes life attributes.**

THE BA GUA

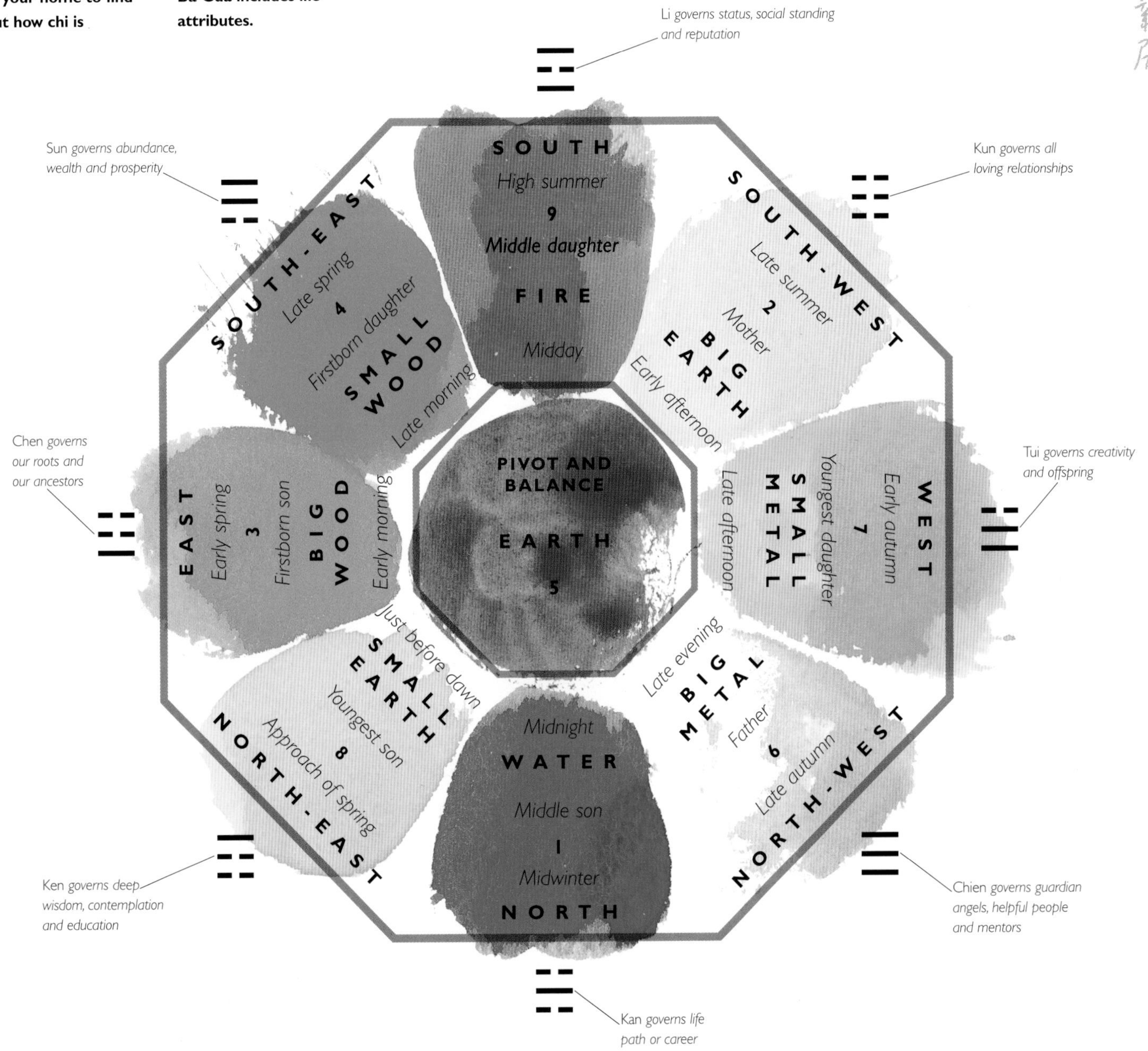

Li governs status, social standing and reputation

Sun governs abundance, wealth and prosperity

Kun governs all loving relationships

Chen governs our roots and our ancestors

Tui governs creativity and offspring

Ken governs deep wisdom, contemplation and education

Chien governs guardian angels, helpful people and mentors

Kan governs life path or career

SOUTH
High summer
9
Middle daughter
FIRE
Midday

SOUTH-EAST
Late spring
4
Firstborn daughter
SMALL WOOD
Late morning

SOUTH-WEST
Late summer
2
Mother
BIG EARTH
Early afternoon

EAST
Early spring
3
Firstborn son
BIG WOOD
Early morning

PIVOT AND BALANCE
EARTH
5

WEST
Early autumn
7
Youngest daughter
SMALL METAL
Late afternoon

NORTH-EAST
Approach of spring
8
Youngest son
SMALL EARTH
Just before dawn

NORTH-WEST
Late autumn
6
Father
BIG METAL
Late evening

NORTH
Midnight
1
Middle son
WATER
Midwinter

BELOW **An absent space in your home will affect the space that falls immediately before it on the Ba Gua, by making it become blocked or overloaded.**

The versions of the Ba Gua printed on these pages are ideal for people who have just begun Feng Shui work. They also incorporate the trigrams (shown surrounding the central Yin and Yang symbol), in case you wish to study the *I Ching* more closely in the future. The trigrams are three-tiered sets of unbroken and broken lines, denoting the way Yin and Yang meet to create chi. Each trigram symbolizes several things. For example, the trigram made up of three unbroken lines is called *Chien (see page 125)*, and is often associated with male energy. It symbolizes heaven and the sky, its element is known as big metal, its number is 6, and its direction is north-west.

The Ba Gua also uses numbers, times of the day, seasons, colours, life attributes, and the energetic contribution of family members, to describe the qualities of a space. This does not imply that one part of a space should be used only by one family member – it simply indicates the kind of energy in a space that could be described in terms of a particular kind of person.

Not all schools of Feng Shui apply the same methods for using the Ba Gua. For example, some practitioners advocate standing in the middle of the home and using a compass to ascertain how to position the Ba Gua over a floor plan of the living space. The method used here, however, involves aligning your main door with the northern sectors of the Ba Gua.

RIGHT **Drawing a floor plan of your home will enable you to identify the missing areas, and the protruding parts, which need attention.**

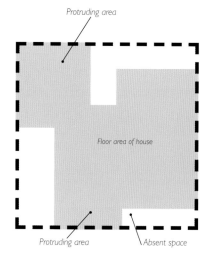

Protruding area

Floor area of house

Protruding area

Absent space

HOW TO USE THE BA GUA

■ Draw a floor plan of your home, as accurately to scale as possible.

■ Copy the Ba Gua on to tracing paper *(see page 125)*.

■ Line up the N, NE or NW sectors of the Ba Gua with the front door of your home. You will now be able to see how each part of your home relates to a different part of your life.

■ You can also lay the whole Ba Gua over a single room by lining up the main door of the room with the northern sectors of the Ba Gua. In this case, each area of the room will correspond to a different part of your life.

■ If you have a garden, you can map it by aligning the garden's main entrance or gate with the northern sectors of the Ba Gua.

挑選新居

LOOKING AT THE OVERALL PICTURE

The shape of the floor plan determines the chi in your home. Square or rectangular homes are most conducive to good Feng Shui; L-shapes, U-shapes, and protruding extensions are less auspicious. In order to remedy protruding areas and absent spaces, a more suitably shaped space has to be built up symbolically in some way. If the irregularly shaped part of the home projects into the garden, it is fairly easy to think of appropriate garden design that will 'round the whole'. Building a terrace, patio or loggia would be one possibility, while adding plants, containers and garden furniture is another.

Inside the home, remedy the areas adjacent to the absent space. First, empower the area immediately before the absent space. If this area is a fire-dominated space, then boost that element with striking flame colours, attention to horizontal planes in the interior design, and objects, pictures and patterns that reflect the highly active, sociable and enlightening nature of fire. Pay particular attention to the quality of daylight and artificial light the room enjoys.

According to the Ba Gua (see page 125), if the area before the absent space is fire, the element of the absent space will be earth: acknowledge it more strongly than usual, with earth colours, shapes and design (see page 21). On the other side of the absent space is the metal sector, and here we will almost certainly find depletion. It would be worth creating an earth energy in this room to nourish the metal (see pages 28–29), such as by using a powerful yellow or terracotta colour (or a combination of these colours), and allowing the room to absorb the expression of abundant resources that earth energy suggests. If the earth energy is balanced, metal energy will find good expression without too much effort on your part. Ensure that the furnishings are well ordered in this room.

Some consultants recommend the use of mirrors to correct absent space, but mirrors are one of the most powerful chi boosters you can use, and should only be used with care. If you want to try it, place a mirror on the wall dividing the absent space from the space before it, so that the mirror faces into the room immediately before the absent space. If this is not possible, consider using a smaller mirror on the wall between the absent space and the room following it. In this case, the mirror should face into the room that follows the absent space. Choose a mirror that is new, framed and of an appropriate shape and size for the job. For example, a square mirror, which represents earth energy, would be an excellent Feng Shui remedy for the example given above. An absent space will reflect and aggravate an imbalance right through the home, so boost the affected element throughout your living space, especially the garden.

BELOW **An** absent space can be corrected with the use of mirrors and by increasing the power of the spaces that fall immediately before and after it on the **Ba Gua**. Look up the corresponding elements on the **Ba Gua**. Whichever elements are needed should be boosted, so that the absent space does not reflect and aggravate an imbalance throughout the rest of the home or workspace.

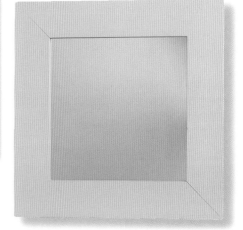

MAKING THE CONNECTION

It is normally true that whatever is revealed by relating a floor plan to the Ba Gua will be repeated, like a pattern, over and over throughout the home. In other words, if when checking individual room shapes against the Ba Gua, you discover an absence in one area, you may well find it recurs. It will also be reflected in your lifestyle and personal health.

As your knowledge of the Ba Gua increases, you will be able to see how deficiencies in your ability to hold chi in your body (creating specific weaknesses and symptoms) coincide with deficiencies in associated areas of your life and your environment. The connections between your spirit, emotions, physical body and outer body (your home) will be there for you to see. It is these connections that enable the Feng Shui follower to make diagnoses and prescribe remedies that will change his or her life on every level.

For example, the absent space we considered earlier, where there was a lack of earth energy (see page 127), is likely to be found in the home of a family or individual whose main challenge is the creation of successful relationships. The occupants may find it difficult to feel centred and secure, and I would also expect food to be a big issue for them in some way. If women are living in the building, I would expect them to be experiencing problems with their health, especially with their immune systems. Men would be having difficulties getting in touch with the feminine energy in their nature, and work would almost certainly be required on their relationship with their mother. In fact, in a space like this, mothering would be a big issue all round. The diagnosis could go on and on, becoming increasingly more detailed and precise.

IDENTIFYING A PATTERN

It is often interesting to look at the floor plans of all the places you have lived in and see if it is possible to identify a pattern, and whether or not it is changing over time. We manifest the space that we need in order to learn particular lessons at different times in life, so using the Ba Gua in this way becomes an invaluable tool for keeping us healthy in body and spirit.

ABOVE **If you have an absent space that falls in the area of deep wisdom and education on the Ba Gua, put a beautiful piece of sculpture or some powerful stones in the space to give the energy a boost.**

However, there is far more we can do than just defining absent space. For example, a projection in a building will identify an overuse of something, an emphasis that needs to be noted and, if extreme, corrected. A projection in an area represented by wood, for example, would warrant a check of the overall wood energy in the house. Is there too much emphasis on 'getting it right', on planning and controlling? Are the occupants often irritable and edgy, resorting to sarcasm or shouting? To remedy this, burn off some of the wood energy by injecting fire into the space, and reduce the water energy (because water nourishes wood). It is often more beneficial to work with the productive and shaping cycles *(see page 21)* rather than manipulating just one element.

When you are looking at your floor plan, look also at the areas where you collect clutter, as well as those that are more neglected or harder to get right. You can then focus on these rooms, considering their individual shape in terms of the Ba Gua because, as mentioned earlier, the Ba Gua can also be laid over the floor plan of a single room. The difficult areas of individual rooms add to the general picture and, by remedying these problems, as well as those of the home overall, you will have another opportunity for success.

To give an example, if an absent space on the plot or in the building falls in the area of deep wisdom, contemplation and education on the Ba Gua, you may find that looking at the room you use for study and reflection will echo that absence with a neglected area corresponding to the same position on the Ba Gua. Remedying that area of the room will boost any remedy you make to the overall living space. On this occasion, an effective treatment would be to place a beautiful piece of sculpture, or a powerful stone, crystal or rock, in the room. You could also put up a picture that for you symbolizes a place where you would be able to develop or transform your inner life and learning processes.

It is important, however, not to make your home into a living shrine to the dictates of Feng Shui. Space should be designed around an instinctive appreciation of what is right, rather than a prescribed formula, however much we hope to be able to guarantee success. If the space feels right, it will be doing exactly the right things for you at that time, however irregular its shape.

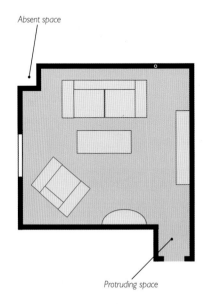

Absent space

Protruding space

ABOVE **A problem revealed by the Ba Gua in one part of the floor plan may be repeated throughout the home.**

If a pattern begins to surface, it may be giving you an important message about a particular area of your life that needs attention.

BELOW **Whether a room functions better as a sitting room, bedroom or kitchen will depend upon the direction it is facing and the kind of chi that enters it.**

COMPASS DIRECTIONS

Once you feel confident that you know how to use the system of compass directions on the Ba Gua, you should ascertain the compass direction with which your home is aligned.

Stand outside your front door, with your back towards the house, and your compass held horizontally in front of you. Read off which direction your home faces. It is important to be standing away from large metal objects, for example cars, when you take the reading. If your front door faces west, then you have a west-facing home. You can also take a reading for a particular room. For example, if the main windows in the room face west, then you can say that it is a west-facing room.

Different directional energies will have particular effects on our homes. By directional energies, we mean the quality of chi brought to us from each compass direction. It is preferable for a home to be aligned a few degrees off directly south, north, east or west. Once you have ascertained the compass direction for your home or a certain room, you can check the effects of the related directional energy and work out why things may be as they are in that space.

NORTH

The energy from the north brings a stillness that allows us to be nurtured and transformed on the deepest level. North-facing homes attract and store the chi that is vital to life. They are adaptable, fluid places, and profoundly powerful.

When out of balance, north-facing homes can become gloomy, depressing and cold, where dormancy becomes inertia, and stored chi becomes blocked. To correct this imbalance, add fluidity of shape and texture to an affected room or the whole home, softening disjointed lines, furnishings and design with sleek patterns and shapes that flow between the spaces. Increase wood chi to keep the northern energy circulating. North-facing rooms are excellent for bedrooms or places of relaxation, but are often neglected. A north-facing home would make an ideal retreat for writing a novel or finishing a symphony. Not always ideal as a long-term residence, a north-facing home can offer respite and support where other spaces have failed to help a person to heal.

NORTH-EAST

Often seen as a gateway to other realms, north-east is considered to be a spiritually highly charged direction. Valued because of its contribution to the etheric plane, this direction's energy is highly unstable because of its concentration at this level. It is well balanced by the dynamic with its polar opposite, the deeply centred south-west. Energy from the north-east is able to ignite the first intention of a return to life after a long hibernation, and make manifest the idea of rebirth.

A room aligned with this direction may appear unnaturally still, but do not be deceived, because energetically it will be a highly charged place full of the potential for movement and change. These qualities will make it an ideal place for a study, or for spiritual practices. Put a laundry room here and you will create a very volatile energy; put a bedroom here, and a dream diary will be an essential accessory.

It is not often advised to choose a home that faces north-east, and if you find yourself living in one, be prepared to get used to the most unexpected happenings. A small Ba Gua-shaped mirror inscribed around its edge with the trigrams, and attached to the top of your porch or front gate, may make life a little more stable.

EAST

The energy that we receive from the east will enliven and invigorate us. Often a little startling in its exuberance, energy from the east is capable of shocking us into action. The great wake-up call from the east will activate even the dullest space, penetrate the toughest armour, and get us moving onwards and upwards in the most direct fashion.

This uplifting energy is beneficial for many homes and rooms. East-facing homes will give people a good start in life or rekindle the energy of a couple entering retirement. They make excellent family homes, and will benefit babies, children and the elderly. Not always good spaces for holiday homes or for entertaining guests, they are none the

RIGHT **Y**ou will find that objects are easily lost and engagements forgotten in a south-east facing room that has a chi imbalance.

less cheerful, nurturing spaces for long-term use, and would be an ideal choice if bought to live in for life.

An east-facing room would be ideally suited to a kitchen, where the rising energy would help to create healing food for growth and renewal. An east-facing room can also be used for the later stages of convalescence, or even as an office for an aspiring business person.

If you are looking for a place in your garden to put a pond or water feature, or even a pool, then look to the east. Water in this area will boost positive chi, but avoid it if it means adding a lot of water too close to the back of your home.

SOUTH-EAST

The energy from this direction brings the potential for future fulfilment. It is high-powered and high-spirited, but can easily be thrown out of balance. Homes facing south-east enjoy the vigour of the east (but softened), and all the promise of the south. If neglected, it will spiral into chaos, where objects go missing and engagements are forgotten. South-east homes suit established couples and families, or single people who enjoy good living and thrive on change and opportunity. A south-east-facing room would make a good breakfast room or meeting room, but avoid using it for entertaining or relaxing in the evening. Use it as an office only if you can concentrate easily.

ABOVE **I**f you are looking for a place to build a pool or add a water feature, choose a spot that faces east. Water, in this direction, will boost positive energy and keep it moving.

RIGHT **A south-facing room is ideal for parties, excitement and passion, but not so good if your priority is a night's rest. South is a good direction for an art gallery or a business that needs to achieve a higher profile.**

SOUTH

Traditionally, a south-facing home is considered the ultimate Feng Shui catch. If you live in a south-facing home, you may enjoy a very high profile in the community. Everything you do could find its way into the public domain very quickly so, famous or infamous, you will need to be prepared to reveal all.

Fortunes may change rapidly in a south-facing home and, if life as a roller-coaster ride is what you enjoy, then this is the place for you. Do not expect to remain in long-term relationships in this home, however – you will need to keep on your toes if you are to stay with a partner. A south-facing property would be a good home to buy in your middle age – it would put a spark into your life. Better still, rent the place and it will be easier to move on once you have had your fun.

A south-facing room will enliven the dullest person. Make a bedroom there if you are looking for excitement and passion rather than rest. South-facing rooms are also good places to put the office of a business that needs to increase its public profile and become better known. It will also be a good space for a party if you remove all the furniture. When the dust settles and everything calms down, you will no doubt realize you have made some fairly dramatic discoveries. Flashes of enlightenment will be the product of time spent facing south.

SOUTH-WEST

If your home faces south-west, look out of your window: any obscurity here will not serve you well. Women, especially mothers, should keep this direction bright. Do not let a room facing south-west fall into disrepair or become filled with junk. If unobstructed, the energy from this direction will keep you healthy in mind and body.

A south-west facing home with good phoenix energy will help anyone whose own mothering fell short. It will replenish a need for nurturing that is difficult to find after childhood. A male single parent would also find life easier here.

Some Feng Shui practitioners are nervous of recommending homes that face south-west, because the energy is said to be unstable. But if your home faces south-west, you are lucky. Past wounds heal in this space. Do not add unsteadying features, such as water inside the home or outside. Instead, add wonderful, stabilizing floors and dazzling textures.

BELOW **The south-west brings energy that will support you and keep you healthy physically, mentally and emotionally. Its nurturing quality is particularly beneficial for those people who lacked a mother's love in childhood.**

South-west facing rooms can be a tonic for people who have had a lot of challenges to face in life. They make excellent living rooms, both for entertaining or enjoying alone. If your bedroom faces south-west, add good quality window coverings to keep things calm. I would hesitate to put a nursery in this direction, and a study here would not be good for research.

NORTH-WEST

A home that faces north-west will help you to gain control of your life and to make the best use of your time and resources. Making important decisions and harnessing suitable talents for future use will be easier in a space like this. North-west facing homes can appear uninspiring from the outside, even austere or drab, but once you are inside and occupied in an activity, you will sense what they have to offer. If you are invited to stay, take any outstanding jobs with you – you may get more work done in a weekend than you would have done in a week at home.

Choose combinations of blues and yellows, and lines that flow and draw the eye downwards or towards solid structures. Be wary of clutter collecting in corners, along walls and behind doors. Avoid having too many dried flowers or seashells. Keep your stock of dried and preserved foods to a minimum, especially dried beans and tinned and

ABOVE **In a house that faces north-west, preserved foods should be kept to a minimum. Replace dried herbs with fresh growing ones in pots that you can put on a bright windowsill.**

frozen foods. Instead eat more fresh food, although it means you have to shop more frequently, and generally increase your consumption of fresh fruit and vegetables, especially if the kitchen faces north-west. Replace dried herbs with growing ones, placed on a bright windowsill.

In the bathroom, again keep stocks of toiletries low, and avoid buying in bulk. Keep the fixtures and paintwork clean and fresh, and avoid having lots of mirrors. Aim for a clear, easy to maintain room. Avoid over-fussy details in the decor and design; watery shapes and images are fine, but keep them well balanced with a feeling of warmth and sunshine.

A north-west room would make a good office, particularly for doing administration, bookkeeping and accounts, or somewhere to store things for infrequent use. It would also make a good bedroom for someone who has difficulty sleeping.

LEFT **A room that faces west should be colourful. It is perfect for relaxation at the end of a tiring day, or for more leisurely and creative pursuits.**

WEST

If you want a home that will let you do things you never had time for before, choose one that faces west. If you have done well in the early part of your life, and want to be a little less active but more creative and leisurely, then cultivate the energy to the west of your home. Just keep it clutter-free and colourful, and it will serve you well. Cut down or thin a few trees, lower fences, and clear any paths. Remove any under-performing items, such as plants, inside and outside. If your home faces west, do not insult it with beige interiors, whitewash or the palest of pastels: let it brim with colour and life. West-facing rooms will allow you to relax and unwind, and are perfect for evening entertaining, dining or games, so give them a new lease of life. In this location a billiard room or library would work well, or a conservatory facing the garden, to enable you to enjoy the last of the day's sun and unwind in anticipation of an evening's entertainment. Avoid sleeping in a west-facing bedroom beyond middle age, however, because it will not give you the rising energy you will need. Likewise, a child may suffer if his or her playroom is placed in this direction. Such a room would, however, help to calm an overactive child.

RIGHT **Traditional
Feng Shui
practitioners devised
a way of mapping
energy changes in
time as well as space.
This has enabled
us to use simple
numerological
calculations to create
an astrological chart.**

FENG SHUI ASTROLOGY

Feng Shui is a study of space and time, and if you wish to pursue your Feng Shui studies and practice in more depth, you need to find a way of charting the changes in chi over time. These cyclical changes alter the energy from one moment to another and have been plotted by people as diverse as astrologers, mariners and farmers. These people are interested in the cyclical movements of chi and how to predict them.

It is because of the predictable nature of these chi movements that we can make some calculations and state, with confidence, the quality that chi is expected to have at any one time, or will have had at a particular point in the past. Feng Shui practitioners are therefore able to say that a house built, or a person born, at a specific time will have certain characteristics or features.

HOW TO FIND YOUR PERSONAL NUMBER

Personal numbers can give us additional insights into our energetic make-up, and enable us to use the information in our environment to improve our wellbeing and quality of life.

1 For the purposes of this system, all years begin on 4th February and end on 3rd February, so people born between 1st January and 3rd February will need to use the preceding year. For example, if you were born on 20th January, 1964, your year of birth will become 1963 for the purpose of these calculations.

2 Add up all the digits of the year of your birth. For example, 1956 would be calculated as follows: $1 + 9 + 5 + 6 = 21$.

3 If the resulting figure is more than 10, add all the digits again until they reach a figure of nine or less. For example, $2 + 1 = 3$.

4 Subtract this figure from 11, so $11 - 3 = 8$.

5 The number you arrive at will be your personal number. In this case, the number would be 8.

Now look for your personal number on the Ba Gua (see *page 125*), and locate the corresponding element. For example, if your personal number is 8, your element will be earth.

RIGHT **If you are**
suffering from
frustration and an
inability to progress
at work or to move
forward in life,

increase the water
energy in the relevant
part of your space. To
find the correct area,
refer to the Ba Gua
on page 125.

桃遷新居

ASTROLOGICAL ANALYSIS

By looking at a person's date of birth, a Feng Shui practitioner can reach an understanding of the way a designated space will affect that person. The practitioner will be able to say that a person born in any one year will have related characteristics, and should therefore live in a particular kind of home facing a certain direction, designed in such a way as to support his or her energy, and should move only in specific directions and at times or dates that the practitioner will recommend.

This kind of astrological analysis can be used to throw light on why events are unfolding in a particular way for a person, and what can be done to help. It adds a new dimension to the work we have been doing in this book, and will come easily to those of you who have already become used to working with chi, the five transforming elements and the Ba Gua. Feng Shui astrology hinges on exactly these same principles.

The process relies on the ability to work with the numbers one to nine, and to translate our findings into the five transforming elements. Using some simple calculations, we can arrive at an astrological chart that will help us to choose the right time to move home, in which direction, and the arrangements to make. However, none of these findings should overrule the assessment we have already made in our initial work to heighten our awareness of chi. These new calculations are there simply to add another layer to the story, and are the result of the helpful input and experience of fellow Feng Shui practitioners.

In order to make the new calculations, you will first need to find your personal number (see opposite). Once you have found it, and located the corresponding element on the Ba Gua (see page 125), look again at the productive cycle of elements (see page 21), and see which elements support you. You can then use the elements to help you in specific ways. For example, if you feel tired and depleted, boost the relevant elements in your space. If you feel blocked, stuck or frustrated, give your energy an outlet by adding the appropriate element to your space. You could build on this by adding the supporting element in the productive cycle, so if you need more fire energy, increase the wood chi, because wood feeds fire. If you are a metal energy person and suffer from immune system deficiencies or asthma, you will need more earth energy to support your vitality. If you also feel frustrated at work and unable to move forward in life, boost the overall water energy of the space. If many of these problems seem to stem from a lack of opportunities to express yourself in childhood, use wood chi to get your deep creative energy moving and to give you the impetus you need.

Using a personal number to help set up a supportive space can become a complicated business, so keep things simple by using it only to add to any assessments you have already made, rather than making it the determining factor in your diagnosis and selection of remedies. If you decide to pursue your study of Feng Shui astrology further, you will be able to build on the information the personal number gives you in such a way as to enable you to structure a greater part of your work around it.

10 choosing a new home

TOP 10 QUESTIONS

The house we want to buy has a history of couples moving in and then splitting up. Could this affect us?

Yes. The history of a house tends to repeat itself. Find out how the Feng Shui of the house contributed to that situation, and remedy it, if possible, before you move in. The house will be able to help you diagnose exactly what is happening in your relationship and which areas you need to work on.

If I use the Ba Gua to assess my space, I find that I do not want to put things like dustbins or compost heaps anywhere. What do you suggest?

Functional items need to be where they are useful. Put the bin in the most practical place. Empty it regularly and keep it clean and all will be well. As for the compost heap, it is a bit like the garden's food store, so if it is well kept and nourished it will do well wherever it is.

I made a floor plan of my new home, but it is an awkward shape and doesn't fit the Ba Gua very well. Someone told me that I could 'square it off' to make it an easier fit. Is this correct?

No, small additions to the floor plan will place an emphasis on those areas of your home and your life. They will also disguise where your home protrudes, and the excess of energy that these protrusions suggest.

I have been told that I can line up the Ba Gua with the centre of a house by taking compass readings. Is this right?

This is a different way of using the Ba Gua and belongs to a different system of Feng Shui called the Compass School. It is not incorrect, but it would be confusing to mix systems so it has not been included in this book (see page 126).

桃選新居

Each time we find a house something prevents us from buying it. What is going on?

The signs are that the type of place you are seeking would not be right for you. Try making two lists: one should show what you want from your new home, and the other should reflect only what you actually need. Compare the two, and your question should be answered. You will then be able to redirect your search in a more appropriate direction.

I have looked at my past homes and found that the same areas of the Ba Gua are missing in each one. Is this a coincidence?

No, this is very common. When such a pattern exists, we can often trace it, or clues of it, right back to the house we were brought up in. Once you have identified the pattern, you can take steps to remedy it, or move to a new space that does not display this pattern.

According to the Ba Gua, the toilet of the flat I want to buy is situated in the wealth sector. What does this mean?

Your finances could 'go down the drain'! Add red to the room to stop the draining away of chi in this area. If there is room, a tall, upward thrusting plant will also help hold onto vital chi. You are basically creating fire energy and feeding it with wood.

The kitchen is located in the marriage area of our new home. What does this signify?

It depends on how much you use your kitchen and how well designed it is. It may be a good opportunity to improve your relationship. Pay special attention to this room, and use warm earth colours for the walls and perhaps terracotta tiles for the floor. Fire and water should not be mixed, so keep the cooker and sink separate.

My house has four floors. Should I treat each floor separately and lay the Ba Gua over each one?

The entire plot and ground floor are the most important areas. If you want to look at the upstairs of your home, treat the top of the stairs as the front door, and align the Ba Gua accordingly.

I use my garage as a workshop. Can I lay the Ba Gua over a floor plan of it?

You can lay the Ba Gua over any space, including your garage and any other workplaces. Be careful not to sleep directly above a garage, however, because it will not support your energy levels.

glossary

A

'Absent space' An area of the Ba Gua that is not represented in the home; it suggests a deficiency of chi in that place, and requires a remedy.

B

Ba Gua An eight-sided diagram that represents nine paths in space and time; it is used to help interpret how chi manifests itself in the universe.

C

Chen This trigram governs where we come from, our roots and our ancestors; its direction is east and its element is big wood.

Chi The invisible breath of energy, or life force, that pervades everything in the universe.

Chien This trigram governs the presence of helpful people and mentors; its direction is north west and its element is big metal.

D

Directional energy The quality of chi that emanates from each compass direction.

Dragon This animal represents the energy of the east and the element wood.

E

Earth Earth energy represents relationships, nurturing, the ability to be centred, and resourcefulness; it is associated with natural earth colours and with the central direction.

East energy This is enlivening and invigorating, and shocks us into action.

Elements In Chinese belief five elements (earth, wood, metal, water and fire) are associated with Feng Shui; they symbolize certain actions, conditions of the mind and seasons.

F

Feng Shui The traditional Chinese system (literally meaning 'wind/water') of harmonizing with the environment by balancing its energy patterns.

Fire Fire energy represents action, enlightenment, self-esteem and public status; it is associated with flame colours and with the direction of south.

I

I Ching Also known as the *Book of Changes*, the *I Ching* is the famous Chinese classic that contains much of the basis of Feng Shui theory.

K

Kan This trigram governs life path or career prospects; its direction is north and its element is water.

Ken This trigram governs wisdom, contemplation and education; its direction is north-east and its element is known as small earth.

Kun This trigram governs all loving relationships; its direction is south-west and its element is big earth.

L

Li This trigram governs status, social standing and reputation; its direction is south and its element is fire.

 M

Metal Metal energy represents order, structure, leisure and pleasure, and creativity; it is associated with white, silver and gold, and with the direction of west.

'Mouth of Chi' A title given to the front, or main, door of a house, illustrating its importance in directing chi inside the building and feeding the environment.

 N

North-east energy This energy is extremely unstable, but it is also highly charged spiritually.

North energy This brings stillness and enables us to be nurtured and transformed.

North-west energy This allows us to gain control of our lives and put time and resources to the best uses.

 P

Personal number A number specific to each person, based on a person's date of birth, that enables additional insights into personality traits and lifestyle.

Phoenix This bird represents the energy of the south and the element fire.

Poison arrow A straight or sharp structure, from which chi bounces off at an angle; it is associated with ill fortune and creates harmful energy.

 P

Productive cycle In this cycle water nurtures wood, which feeds fire, which makes earth, which creates metal, which in turn holds water.

 S

Shaping cycle In this cycle wood consumes earth, which dams water, which extinguishes fire, which melts metal, which in turn cuts wood.

Snake This animal represents the energy of the centre and the element earth.

South-east energy This is high-powered, bringing the potential for future fulfilment, but it can easily be thrown out of balance.

South energy This is changeable and enlivening.

South-west energy This is unstable, but also healing and acts as a tonic.

Sun This trigram governs abundance, wealth and prosperity; its direction is south-east and its element is small wood.

 T

Tiger This animal represents the energy of the west and the element metal.

Tortoise This animal represents the energy of the north and the element water.

Trigram A three-tiered set of broken and unbroken lines that symbolizes the way in which Yin and Yang meet to create chi.

Tui This trigram governs creativity and offspring; its direction is west and its element is small metal.

 W

Water Water energy represents contemplation and quiet; it is associated with blue and black, and with the direction of north.

West energy This is relaxing and creative energy.

Wood Wood energy represents growth, development, new ideas and planning; it is associated with the colour green, and with the direction of east.

 Y

Yang Creative energy, perceived as active, masculine, hot and sharp; its complementary opposite is Yin and, together with Yin, it is present in all things in life.

Yin Receptive energy, perceived as passive, feminine, soft and cold; its complementary opposite is Yang and, together with Yang, it is present in all things in life.

further reading

Master Lam Kam Chuen
The Feng Shui Handbook
Gaia, 1995

Dianne M. Connelly
Traditional Acupuncture:
The Law of the Five Elements
The Centre for Traditional Acupuncture, 1975

Stephen L. Karcher and
Rudolph Ritsema
I Ching
Element Books, 1994

Karen Kingston
Clear Your Clutter with Feng Shui
Piatkus, 1998

Karen Kingston
Creating Sacred Space with Feng Shui
Piatkus, 1996

Mishio Kushi
Nine Star Ki
One Peaceful World, 1991

Denise Linn
Sacred Space Clearing and Enhancing the
Energy of Your Home
Rider, 1995

Jan Sandifer
Feng Shui Astrology
Piatkus, 1997

Stephen Skinner
The Living Earth Manual
Arkana, 1989

William Spear
Feng Shui Made Easy
Thorsons, 1995

Gerry Thompson
Feng Shui Astrology for Lovers
Sterling, 1998

Lao Tsu
Tao Te Ching
Wildwood House Ltd., 1992

Richard Wilhelm (trans.)
The I Ching or Book of Changes
Routledge and Kegan Paul, 1968

R. L. Wing
The Illustrated I Ching
HarperCollins, 1987

Takashi Yoshikawa
The Ki
St Martin's Press, 1986

useful addresses

AUSTRALASIA

Feng Shui Design Studio
PO Box 7788
Bondi Beach
Sydney 2026
Australia
Tel: 61 2 9365 7877
Fax: 61 2 9365 7847

Feng Shui Consultants
PO Box 34160
Birkenhead
Auckland
New Zealand
Tel: 64 9 483 7513

Feng Shui Society of Australia
c/o North Sydney Shopping World
PO Box 6416
Sydney 2060
Australia

GREAT BRITAIN

Feng Shui Association
31 Woburn Place
Brighton BN1 9GA
Tel/fax: 44 1273 693844

Feng Shui Company
Ballard House
37 Norway Street
Greenwich
London SE10 9DD

Feng Shui Foundation (Jane Butler-Biggs)
PO Box 1640
Hassocks
East Sussex BN6 9ZT
E-mail: fengshui.foundation@virgin.net

Feng Shui Society
377 Edgware Road
London W2 1BT
Tel: 07050–289 2000
Web site: www.fengshuisociety.org.uk

Feng Shui Network International
8 King's Court
Pateley Bridge
Harrogate
North Yorkshire HG3 5JW
Tel: 44 7000 336474
Fax: 44 1423 712869

The Geomancer
The Feng Shui Store
PO Box 250
Woking
Surrey GU21 1YJ
Tel: 44 1483 839898
Fax: 44 1483 488998

NORTH AMERICA

Earth Design
PO Box 530725
Miami Shores
FL 33153
Tel: 1 305 756 6426
Fax: 1 305 751 9995

Feng Shui Designs Inc.
PO Box 399
Nevada City
CA 95959
Tel/fax: 1 800 551 2482

The Feng Shui Institute of America
PO Box 488
Wabasso
FL 32970
Tel: 1 561 589 9900
Fax: 1 561 589 1611

Feng Shui Warehouse
PO Box 6689
San Diego
CA 92166
Tel: 1 800 399 1599/1 619 523 2158
Fax: 1 800 997 9831/1 619 523 2165

index

acknowledgments

AUTHOR'S ACKNOWLEDGMENTS

I would like to thank Terry and Rita Butler for making space available for me in their lives and hearts and for giving me enduring unconditional love, my guide and teacher for recognising me and showing me how to heal, my students everywhere, but especially my nine apprentices, in whose teaching I have learnt just how deep and far-reaching our pool of wisdom is. Above all I would like to thank Rob Butler-Biggs for his absolute faith in my work and his ability to be always several steps ahead when it mattered most.

The publisher would like to thank the following for help with photography and props:

Helene Adamczewski
Brats, Lewes, East Sussex
Bright Ideas, Lewes, East Sussex
C.H. Seymour Limited, Lewes, East Sussex
Farrago, Lewes, East Sussex
Furniture 151, Lewes, East Sussex
Geoffrey Aldred (stonemason), Lewes.
East Sussex

PHOTOGRAPHIC CREDITS

Abode, UK: pp.13tr, 15tl&r, 15br, 25, 86bl, 88 both, 115r, 117, 126, 130, 131, 132b
The Garden Picture Library: pp.39r, 97t&r, 98 all, 99, 100 all, 101, 102, 103, 104, 105, 135
The Image Bank, London: pp. 22tr, 32t both, 52t, 65t
Interior Archive, London: pp. 15cl (James Mortimer), 24cr, 42bl (Christopher Simon Sykes)
Houses and Interiors, London: pp. 53tl, 84
The Stock Market, London: pp. 6b, 8bl, 9b, 14t, 19t, 35r all, 36, 39t, 44bl, 48b, 50b, 56bl, 57b, 58, 75b, 78l, 111t, 123b, 132t
Elizabeth Whiting Associates: pp. 9tr, 46t
Tony Stone Images: pp. 11b, 23, 35tl, 45b, 57t, 62, 67r, 79, 82, 93, 113r, 114